he Landlord as Scapegoat

The Landlord as Scapegoat

Keith Lehrer

The Fraser Institute
Vancouver, British Columbia, Canada

Excerpts from *The House of All Sorts* by Emily Carr were reprinted with the permission of Stoddart Publishing Co. Limited, 34 Lesmill Rd., Don Mills, Ontario, Canada.

Canadian Cataloguing in Publication Data

Lehrer, Keith (Keith Akiva)
The landlord as scapegoat

Includes bibliographical references.
ISBN 0-88975-114-5

1. Landlords. I. Fraser Institute (Vancouver, B.C.)
II. Title.
HD7288.8L43 1990   333.5'4   C90-091567-6

74876

Printed in Canada.

CONTENTS

FIGURES AND TABLES

PREFACE

The Fraser Institute is widely known throughout Canada as an economic public policy research organization. Indeed, it has been characterized by the *Toronto Star* as "the most notable think tank in Canada articulating the conservative view of economics." This emphasis on economics is correct, because the Institute's research programme is dedicated to the analysis of public policy issues, and the overwhelming majority of its research has been conducted from an economic perspective.

It might appear, then, that the present book is a sharp departure from the publication programme of the Fraser Institute, for *The Landlord as Scapegoat* by Professor Keith Lehrer is a sociological, not an economic, text. However, this book is not as much of a deviation from accepted Institute practice as might first appear, since there are several exceptions to the general rule that economics is the underlying perspective from which all problems are viewed. For example, *Canadian Medicine: A Study in Restricted Entry* by Ronald Hamowy is a historical, not an economic, analysis. Lance Roberts, an eminent Manitoba sociologist, contributed a chapter to *Discrimination, Affirmative Action, and Equal Opportunity* as did Kurt Vonnegut, the celebrated novelist. Further, the Institute has published a six-volume series on religious and ethical issues that features the works of numerous theologians, and half of the authors of *Reaction: The New Combines Investigation Act* are legal scholars and jurists.

As well, *The Landlord as Scapegoat* forms an integral part of the Fraser Institute series on rent control. Lehrer's thesis is that the strife that mars rental housing relations almost always harms the social-psychological-economic position of the landlord. But this friction between landlord and tenant is always exacerbated by rent control, and this is a legislative enactment studied in detail by *Rent Control: A Popular Paradox* (1975) and *Rent Control: Myths and Realities* (1981).

Thanks to Lehrer's unstinting efforts, for the first time in the annals of Canadian sociological research we hear the landlords themselves: their pain, frustration, powerlessness, outrage, and sense of victimization. Turning current sociological and conventional wisdom upside-down, this York University sociologist shows that it is not the landlord who is the master and the tenant, the servant and dependant; rather, to the extent that this relationship describes the housing market at all, the very reverse is much more nearly the case. The landlord is *not* a powerful, almost omnipotent figure. The ability of the small landlord to control his surroundings has been sharply reduced by governments with rent control legislation, by organized tenant groups, and by the false assumption of excessive landlord power exposed in this study.

The terminology in current use is misleading. The phrase "landlord" harkens back to medieval days when the lord of the manor was the master of all he surveyed, and the serfs on his domain were little better than slaves.

Nowadays, the power position of the owner of rental property has atrophied, to say the least, as Lehrer so eloquently shows us. But because of the survival and still current usage of the word "landlord," this reality has been obscured. (For a literary insight into how at least some elements of society see the landlord, see the novel by Ellis Peters, *Death of the Landlords*, London: Macmillan-Headline, 1972.)

It cannot possibly be over-emphasized that the Lehrer analysis applies only to landlord-tenant relations under rent control. To be sure, there will always be some tension between the landlord (you should pardon the expression) and the tenant. Presumably, this dates from the dawn of civilization. But there is no reason to expect this strain to be more deeply entrenched than that which prevails in any other enduring commercial relationship. Employer and employee, exporter and importer, merchant and customer, principal and agent, wholesaler and retailer—they all function with one another under pressure. They all grate one upon the other; they can all, upon occasion, even call for the services of an arbiter or a court of law.

There is an important reason why the stress in any of these situations is no worse than it is: both parties to the arrangement have something to gain from their partners in commerce. This provides the cement that binds them together, however imperfectly, however uncomfortably. Each would experience material loss were it not for the other, and each partner knows this full well.

This situation also applies to landlords and tenants—but only in a free market. The proof is that in the absence of rent control, landlord-tenant relations are no worse than in these other commercial relationships. Who has ever heard, for example, of nasty and vituperative relationships between the owner of the office building and his commercial tenants, or between the shopping centre mall and the merchants who rent space there? Nor are reasonably good landlord-tenant relations confined to commercial and industrial property; they apply to residential units as well, provided only that they go unregulated by rent control. To wit, the relationship between the landlord of a luxury building not subject to regulation and his wealthy tenants is usually as good as or better than that which applies to any other commercial agreement. And this applies as well to the traveller and the motel, hotel, or bed and breakfast emporium that rents a night's lodging. In the case of rent control, however, the cement that would otherwise bind the landlord and tenant to respectful co-operation with each other crumbles away. Now, instead of each seeing the other as a source of mutual benefit, they see each other as a threat to personal and economic welfare.

Typically, the rent controlled landlord would like nothing better than for his tenant to vacate the premises. If so, he could capture a windfall profit, either by converting to condominium status, selling the building, or renting to another tenant at a much higher rate. All his natural entrepreneurial incentives to serve the consumer ("The customer is always right!") are thus perverted by rent control into a steadfast desire to perform as little service as possible. And the tenant, for his part, also finds himself in an adversary position. He cannot offer a higher rent in order to obtain better services, if only because of the fact that such payments, under rent control, are illegal. So the two are at each other's throats in a way that does not apply to any other commercial relationship.

In some communities that have suffered under rent controls for long periods of time, altercations between landlord and tenant have become so prevalent that they have swamped court calendars. Things have come to such a pass that special courts have had to be created to deal with landlord-tenant strife. New York City—where rent controls have been in force since 1941—has the dubious distinction of being the leader in this regard. It has been forced to install special housing courts that deal solely with conflict arising out of rent control provisions.

But we need not resort to U.S. experience to illustrate this phenomenon when there is Canadian evidence available. Consider the following table:

Landlord-Tenant Cases in British Columbia by Fiscal Year

Rent Control in Force	Number of Cases
1978-1979	17,200
1979-1980	22,498
1980-1981	27,749
1981-1982	40,009
1982-1983	43,455
Average	30,182

No Rent Control (as of July 1983)	Number of Cases
1984-1985	3,003
1985-1986	3,918
1986-1987	5,341
1987-1988	5,212
1988-1989	6,618
Average	4,818

Sources: Data for 1978-1979 to 1983-1984 from the Annual Report of the Ministry of Consumer and Corporate Affairs (Office of the Rentalsman), Province of British Columbia; data for 1984-1985 to 1988-89 from the Annual Report of the Ministry of Labour and Consumer Services (Residential Tenancy Branch), Province of British Columbia.

The five years before and after the advent of rent control in British Columbia are revealing in terms of the level of landlord-tenant hostility. During the rent control era, the average annual number of case files opened by the Rentalsman in behalf of disputatious landlords and tenants was 30,182; in the non-rent control period, the equivalent number was 4,818. This represents an 84 percent decline.

Although dramatic, these figures must be interpreted cautiously. They are derived from two different sets of data, which are not fully consistent with one another. Statistics for the earlier period are based on the Rentalsman's calculation of "case files opened"; those for the latter were obtained by adding "applications for arbitration" and "information files opened" as recorded by the Residential Tenancy Branch.

It is impossible to prove that the elimation of rent control was responsible for the striking decrease in belligerence, as there has been no attempt to control other variables that might have independently altered the level of litigiousness between these two groups. Nevertheless, the statistical record suggests that this is what has occurred.

It is possible that these findings understate the case for the hypothesis that rent control exacerbates landlord-tenant hostilities. This is because B.C.'s population grew during these years (it was 2.5 million in 1978, 2.8 million in 1983, and 2.9 million in 1988—B.C. Economic and Statistical Review, table 3.2, 1989), and additional landlord and tenant complaints could be expected to arise from this source alone.

With this overview of the economics of rent control, we now move to a brief summary of the contents of *The Landlord as Scapegoat*.

Chapter 1

Since this book is an analysis of landlords in terms of their power (or absence, thereof), Lehrer provides us with a template of power relationships. This study analyses the increasing loss of landlord control through a taxonomy that breaks power down to the following constituent elements: religious/moral/spiritual, military/coercive/physical, spatial/territorial, traditional/patrimonial, political/judicial/public administrative/legislative, economic/financial/material, socio/cultural, organizational, personal/socio-psychological, informational/technological, decision-making/executive, and occupational. The key, as far as property owners are concerned, is that "tenure of possession is viewed increasingly as giving rise to more legitimate rights than legal ownership" (p. 3).

Chapter 2

According to the usual expectation, if there is one aspect of power in which landlords exceed tenants, it is in terms of the ability to make and enforce economic and financial decisions. However, a wealth of anecdotal evidence—all, unfortunately, that is available to buttress this point—indicates the very opposite. On the one hand there are numerous small landlords, many of them elderly, ethnics, and/or members of visible minority groups, who must struggle to meet mortgage payments on residential dwellings. On the other hand there is a plethora of tenants who own luxury automobiles, "which sprinkle the

x

underground residential parking lots" of buildings subject to rent controls. Often, the leasing costs of these vehicles exceed the apartment rent charged to their owners. In many cases rents constitute less then 10 percent of income. Such tenants can afford summer cottages, world cruise vacations, expensive electronic goods, as well as their fancy cars, because these commodities are purchased with monies that in a more just society might otherwise have gone for rent.

Among the valuable contributions of the Lehrer report are the quotes and cartoons he cites. They dramatically illustrate the widely held view of landlord omnipotence and tenant powerlessness. But there are laws on the books that prohibit "hate literature" against an identifiable group. The cartoons that illustrate this book show the denigration of the landlord, and attest to the fact that this occupation may qualify for the protection of anti-hate legislation. The landlord is depicted as greedy, wealthy, uncaring, scheming, villainous, exploitative, murderous—and worse.

Why this vast level of misinformation? Historically, the landlord *did* oppress tenants. In medieval days the landlord was the clear master and the tenant was the serf. Although several centuries have gone by since those bad old days, and a revolution in commercial relationships has taken place, many members of the media still have not incorporated these changes into their reportorial perspectives.

One indication of the decline of the landlord's territorial-spatial-proprietary power is his exceedingly limited power of eviction. Apart from non-payment of rent or gross destruction of property, it is almost impossible to evict a tenant from property supposedly owned by the landlord.

To highlight the changing power relationships, Lehrer contrasts the homeowner not with his fellow property owning landlord but with the tenant. Now one would think that homeowners are in a far more enviable power position than tenants. After all, the former own property, the latter do not. However, states Lehrer, "those homeowners with mortgages are obliged to make regular payments to mortgage holders, with possibly less chance of sufferance and latitude than in the case of tenants paying rent."

Why the paradox? Answers our author: tenant's organizational advantages outweigh those of homeowners. Residential renters have a ready-made and highly visible adversary (the evil landlord who typically utters, "I've come for the rent the rent the rent, heh heh"), whereas people who own their homes do not. All tenants are affected by common programmes (e.g., rent control), whereas those that impact homeowners, such as high interest charges, affect only those who must renegotiate mortages at any one time, a small fraction of the total. This is why there are full-time professional tenant, but not homeowner, organizers.

Chapter 3

Virtually all writing on housing problems has focused on the plight of the tenant. It is the virtue of the Lehrer study that it redresses the imbalance and focuses on difficulties of landlords, especially the relatively poor ones.

Exhibit "A" in the case attesting to the powerlessness of landlords is the experience of Emily Carr, renowned Canadian artist. She was subjected to loss of standing in the community, treated as a servant by her tenants, and suffered arrears and non-payment of rent, while her mortgage payments were due at the bank. Worse, tenants destroyed her property, and she was even subjected to threats of physical violence.

But her experiences were less injurious than that accorded the typical landlord in Canada today, for she was a member of the white English-speaking non-immigrant elite. In sharp contrast, most small landlords in present day Ontario—where rent controls are still in existence—are immigrants, visible minorities, and persons for whom English is only a second language.

The bureaucratic and judicial runaround that such people are subjected to renders Carr's experiences, however arduous, far less harsh. It is especially outrageous in this age of "human rights," says Lehrer that these powerless immigrant landlords are victimized by discrimination and subjected to treatment that would be vigorously protested, and illegal, were it to occur to any other visible minority group members.

In addition to the Carr case, the author of this book reports on his informal survey of the experiences of ten Toronto landlords (they should be called the Toronto Ten, to indicate their sense of alienation). In a rare display of emotion, they discourse on their travails: the non-paying tenants who refuse to leave, the purposefully damaged apartments, the tenants who lock themselves out at midnight, the threatening phone calls in the small hours of the morning, the actual beatings suffered at the hands of tenants, the array of officious bureaucrats insisting upon repairs on behalf of cheque bouncing tenants—and the refusal of the police to defend their persons or property rights. A cry from the heart, sufficient to emotionally impact all but the most unfeeling of professional tenant activists.

Why do the landlords do it? Are they masochists? According to Professor Lehrer's research, they engage in this activity for the most usual of commercial motivations: the desire to better their economic condition, usually by realizing capital gains. In the event, however, they are usually disappointed. There are rarely operational profits and, says Lehrer, "if rents are constrained through control legislation, so then is the value of property." In the rare exceptional case of actual profits, any "windfall" increase in capital value attracts the undivided attention of voracious tax gatherers. As to the actual bottom line, states our author, "suffice to state here that the average gain (to the small landlord) has been a negative figure."

Our York University professor also takes us on a tour of recent Ontario housing history, analyzing the speculation and house flipping of the early 1970s, the subsequent Landlord and Tenant Act of 1975 which imposed rent controls, the "Cadillac Fairview debacle of the early 1980s, and the Thom Royal Commission of Enquiry (into rental housing).

Chapter 4

It is sometimes said that women, the handicapped, native persons, and visible and ethnic minorities are becoming a new brahmin caste in Canada. Certainly, these historically downtrodden groups have recently been targeted for benefits from a spate of pay equity, reverse discrimination, and "human rights" legislation and judicial findings.

But not if they are landlords.

Lehrer shows that members of visible and ethnic minorities are disproportionally represented amongst the class of small landlords. (Included under this rubric are those, particularly, who own 12 or fewer units, but sometimes extending up to 30 suites, provided that they are concentrated geographically and thus can be managed by one person.)

Despite the widely held notion that most rented property is owned in large blocks by white males, the reality is that much of it is held—in exceedingly small parcels—by Sikhs, Pakistanis, West Indians, Africans and by new arrivals of Greek, Italian, Portuguese, and Chinese extraction. The cultural background of these immigrants often promotes the view that one hasn't really "made it" in the new country unless one owns property. These people naturally gravitate toward rental unit ownership, if only because rent controls heavily, and negatively, impact the capital value of these structures. (Thus, they can afford to buy in.) Lehrer notes that "the experience of dispossession as refugees from a previous country may heighten the psychological need felt to regain tangible property in a new host country. This may help explain the large number of European Jews among the landlord populations of the U.K., the U.S., and possibly Canada" (p. 60).

Another explanation of immigrant affinity for small scale landlording is discrimination and racism. Lehrer states,

> All the normal power bases available to communities—legal, economic, political, and social—were, then, denied the Chinese community and other ethnic minorities. ('No Jews, Negroes or Dogs' was a public notice on Toronto beaches, still remembered by citizens growing up in the 1940s.) So it is not surprising that, despite the drawbacks and vulnerabilities already illustrated, they would cling to small-scale property ownership and renting as a meagre source of income, security, and territorial power (p. 60).

In Lehrer's analysis, rent control may be understood as a thinly disguised modern day form of racism. "This may help explain why the host community has been quick to condemn, has put difficulties in the small landlord's way, and has provided increasingly protective legislation to its predominantly white English-speaking private tenant population" (p. 62).

Nor is paternalism unknown:

> ...the overwhelming majority of the defendants in cases brought by the city housing inspectors (plumbing, electrical, health, etc.) were ethnic immigrants. While in some cases the magistrate was sympathetic, in most his manner was paternalistic. He was white and spoke English with a confident Canadian accent (p. 63).

Similarly, in the U.K. we learn that 98 percent of all legal action against landlords concerns Indians and Pakistanis. This is a clear and present divergence from the way "progressive forces" in this country would wish to see visible minorities treated.

There is no question that such patronizing and discriminatory behaviour would outrage our sensibilities were it to occur in any other context. If a white employer talked down to or singled out immigrant employees in such a manner, there is little doubt that he or she would be brought up on harassment charges forthwith. But with landlords, it would appear, there is a separate standard.

The picture that emerges from Lehrer's analysis of rent control is *not* one of downtrodden, helpless tenants being protected from powerful white landlords; in fact, a reverse of that image, one with victimized landlords and powerful tenants, would be a more truthful representation. Consider the ethnic composition of the Ontario MPPs, the group responsible for the enactment of rent control legislation in the first place. It is very different from that of the small landlord population: "there is not one Portuguese, Spanish, or Greek representative in the assembly, which indicates the paucity of representation of recent southern European immigrant communities. Perhaps even more telling is the absolute lack of representation for blacks, Chinese, Japanese, and East Indians" (p. 65). And a similar breakdown applies to the Ontario police force, the group charged with enforcing rent control legislation.

Chapter 5

Just who are the owners of small amounts of residential rental property in Toronto? Lehrer explores the Landlord Self-Help Centre. This group was set up because "while tenants who were oppressed by landlords could go to one of many government-supported legal aid clinics, landlords had no such place to turn to when they were cheated or exploited by their tenants" (p. 69). In the five-year period studied, this organization came to the aid of 5,628 clients, and the statistical story of this group of people is revealing. For example, while the mother tongue of 71 percent of Torontonians was English, this held true for only 32 percent of landlords. The subject group also had more dependants than average. Of the landlords, 23 percent had three or more dependants, compared to only 15 percent of the general population. As well, the landlords were older (45 percent above age 50) than the general Toronto population (30 percent above age 50). And, most damaging to the case for landlord as rich exploiter, their total income from *all* sources was lower: "52 percent of the LSHC clients declared total incomes from all sources of less than $12,000, while census data show that only 13.98 percent of all families in the Toronto CMA had to contend with such a low level of income..." (p. 77).

Chapter 6

Is the landlord-tenant relationship analogous to the one that characterizes the employer-employee relationship? Does the small landlord occupy the same sociological role of the boss in industrial relations? Not bloody likely. On the contrary, says Lehrer, he occupies a social position more in keeping with those at the bottom of the employment hierarchy:

> The landlord has often been referred to with the introductory epithet 'slum,' and with an image as tainted as a pariah, he has come to be compared to pimps, prostitutes, and other social outcasts (p. 89).

And again:

> Not only does he have to act as bill collector but unless he is quite well off, he will have to fulfil at least some of the functions of janitor—garbage collection, cleaning windows, washing floorways, putting on and taking off storm windows, and other more or less menial and dirty jobs (p. 90).

Chapter 7

The small landlord is popularly seen as a powerful, exploitative villain, and the tenant as a helpless minority in need of governmental largess and protection. (This, in part, explains the acceptability of rent control, despite the dire warnings of virtually the entire economics profession against it.*) But the reality is the polar opposite. The small landlord is likely to be poorer, older, and less powerful than the average person in society, and more likely to be a member of a visible or ethnic minority.

---

* Walter Block and Michael Walker, "Entropy in the Canadian Economics Profession: Sampling Consensus on the Major Issues," *Canadian Public Policy*, vol. XIV, no. 2, June 1988, p. 140, report that only 4.7 percent of all Canadian economists polled on this question disagree with the statement "A ceiling on rents reduces the quantity and quality of housing available."

With this undeserved moral high ground, tenants have been able to abuse landlords with impunity. The stories are legion of rich diamond merchants, lawyers, and other "limousine liberals" who use their rent controlled premises as a *pied à terre* two or three times a month. "It's far cheaper than a downtrodden hotel," says one of them.

Yet government continues to justify this 'Sovietization' of the rental market under the guise of helping "poor tenants." To be sure, there are many impoverished tenants; not all are as rich as the exploiters documented by Lehrer. And, yes, modern democratic societies have indeed mandated that poor people shall be given access to housing. However, Canadians also insist that the poor not starve—but have not found it necessary to impose price controls on McDonald's, Burger King, Safeway, and 7-Eleven. In like manner, rental housing could easily be provided to the less fortunate members of society without vitiating the human rights of yet another denigrated group—small landlords, and indeed, all landlords.

Lehrer's analytic framework applies mainly to the epoch of the late 1970s and early 1980s. This is purposeful, as that was the era of the onset of rent control and its immediate after-effects. These events set the stage for all that was to follow. Little has changed in the ensuing period except, as our author notes (pp. 96-98), that the hypocrisy of rich tenants abusing a rent control system ostensibly set up for the poor has become even more entrenched. This is now a *cause célèbre* in New York City, and Toronto has followed in the footsteps of the Big Apple.

A word about anecdotal evidence. This book is chock-full of stories of actual landlords and tenants. Such anecdotal evidence is rare in the scholarly literature, because it is incapable of statistical and mathematical manipulation. But, as the average person knows full well, there is more to life than the merely quantifiable. Lehrer's sociological analysis gives us accurate appreciation of the landlord-tenant reality. He takes us through the newspapers, the tenant meetings—his pithy cartoons are each worth thousands of words—and when our intellectual travels are complete, we will never look at this area of endeavour in the same way again.

The author of this book has worked independently. The opinions expressed by him, therefore, are his own and do not necessarily reflect the opinions of the members or the trustees of the Fraser Institute.

Walter Block

ABOUT THE AUTHOR

Dr. Lehrer has been on faculty at York University, Toronto, since 1974, where he has taught finance, accounting, and more recently, organization, management, real estate administration, and housing policy. Born in London, England, in 1944, he obtained his first degree in economics at Manchester University in 1964. Thereafter, he pursued a career in professional and management accounting, working for such companies as Shell, ITT, and IBM. He obtained his English F.C.A. and later earned his Canadian C.A. designation after immigrating to Toronto in 1970.

Professor Lehrer obtained his M.A. and Ph.D. in sociology at York University from 1978 to 1984. His current research interests include housing and transportation policies for aging populations. Recent publications include an analysis of the free trade issue and its impact on the last Canadian federal election (*The Nation*, Israel).

CHAPTER 1

Introduction

This study is focused on the role of the small residential landlord in Western society. It is at the same time an attempt to shed light on the role of power in a democratic society, via the workings of the housing sub-system of society, and in particular, its private rental sector.

A comprehensive analysis of power has not been attempted as part of this study. However, a few comments to orient the reader to notions of power utilized in the study may be found helpful. Weber's (1946) concept of legitimacy underpins a great deal of both sociological and political thinking about power. While subsuming the concept of legal-rational authority, legitimacy provides a wider and deeper basis of societal power. One obeys the law not only because one is required to do so (legal authority), and not only because the law appears to follow an appropriate rule of logic (rationality) but also because it feels right and "proper" to do so (legitimate authority). Thus one might explain obeisance to legal-rational power in terms of practicality and expedience in a highly organized society (Presthus 1978). One might explain the power of legitimate authority as residing in the value systems of the society as a whole (Habermas 1976), both reflecting them and helping re-shape them.

For analytical purposes, another way of understanding the role of the landlord in the general social system, unfortunately neglected in the housing literature, is in terms of his or her access to all bases of power. It is possible to split societal power into many components and to develop a fairly lengthy taxonomy, as in figure 1. For the purposes of this study emphasis will be placed on a restricted selection of such power bases, mostly revolving around:

- spatial-territorial power
- political-judicial-public administrative-legislative power (non-coercive elements of government power)
- economic-financial-material power
- organizational power

- personal, socio-psychological, and occupational power
- informational (including media) power
- decision-making and executive power.

The present study may be seen as an attempt to show how the power bases available to the small residential landlord have been weakened progressively, as access to power bases by a majority of private residential tenants has strengthened. This changing power balance, it may be argued, has been supported both by specific acts of the political, judicial, and administrative institutions of the State (political-judicial-public administrative-legislative power), and, perhaps more fundamentally, by undermining the rights of the residential landlord while increasing the rights of the tenant. Thus the Weberian role for legitimacy of authority in society is not negated but underlined by this broader analytical approach.

Figure 1
A Partial Taxonomy of Power Bases[1]

BASE	SOURCES
BLOCK A (pre-industrial)	
1. religious/moral/spiritual	Weber/Durkheim
2. military/coercive/physical	Etzioni
3. spatial/territorial	The Bible/Marx/Rodegard/Bismarck
4. medical	Evans-Pritchard/Goffman/Maxwell
5. traditional/patrimonial	Weber
BLOCK B (industrial)	
6. political/judicial/public/ administrative/legislative	Weber/Machiavelli
7. economic/financial/material	Marx
8. socio-cultural	Homans
9. organizational	Marx/Weber/Perrow
BLOCK C (post-industrial)	
10. personal/socio-psychological	Weber/Goffman/Kafka
11. informational/technological	Galbraith/McLuhan
12. decision-making/executive	Simon
13. occupational	Hughes/Goffman

NOTE: Further classifications of power are explored in note 1, but for purposes of parsimony they have been subsumed in the analysis here under the above categories.

Such a socio-political process might be explained partially by a re-formulation of the rights of property (Macpherson 1978). Possibly tenure of possession is viewed increasingly as giving rise to more legitimate rights than legal ownership (possession thus becomes ultimately nine tenths of the law). It might also be partially explained by the less than perfectly equitable workings of representative democracy. Tenants in urban agglomerations such as New York, London, and more recently, Toronto, are far more numerous than their landlords. Their potential political power is an inherent part of their majority status. Landlords have not only been a minority in this numerical sense; according to the British research of Rex and Moore (1967), of Burney (1967), to some extent the Canadian research of Krohn, Fleming, and Manzer (1979), and the New Zealand research of Lehrer (1984B), in addition to the findings presented in this study, ethnic minorities represent an unduly large proportion of the population making up this minority interest group of private residential landlords. They may therefore have a compounded minority status (eg., a black single mother).

To the extent then that private residential landlords have been ascribed a pariah status in contemporary society, it is appropriate to question the degree to which their aggregate power has been eroded by an admittedly complex social and political process, but one in which a democratic de-legitimization and underprivileged ethnic status have played significant interactive parts. It is to these issues that we now turn.

Notes

1. To these categories others could be added, such as professional, union, media, numerical, class, and community. This list could be extended almost indefinitely, but for purposes of this analysis all of these may be organized under the general taxonomy of power bases outlined in the text. Union power may be considered as the power of an interest group and therefore too specialized to constitute a general power base: its source of total power might be construed to derive from a consortium of our more elemental power bases, chiefly perhaps of bases 6, 7, 8, 9, and 13. (Similar types of analysis can be done for any social group.)

    Although media power can be presented as having had significant impact on changes in the power relations of the major groups in the organization and distribution of housing, it has been subsumed under the power base of information (distributing, collecting, withholding, editing, distorting, etc.).

    Numerical power, the power of large numbers, has been translated in most of the world's societies into political power, via different degrees and types of enfranchisement. Pockets still exist where numbers are ignored and their political power negated (South Africa is perhaps a too-quoted example), though even here the power of numbers is not eliminated but merely overshadowed by a so-far more successful application of other power-bases, notably military-coercive power. (Elsewhere the power of numbers has been used in external politics, e.g., using millions of poorly armed and equipped Russian soldiers in the First and Second World Wars to counter a superior military machine, and the sacrifice of over a quarter million [to date] Iranians and Iraqis, many totally unarmed and at twelve and thirteen years of age, in a largely unpublicized war of attrition. This acts as a gruesome illustration not just of the combined power of religion and coercion even in this age but also of the power to suppress or provide information and media coverage.)

    Numbers, then, may provide a power base, but usually as just one resource within another power base, such as the political, military, or organizational. The political debate of elites and masses would suggest that numbers by themselves are ineffectual as a power base. Work by such diverse authors as Koestler on Roman slaves and Zola on French coal-miners in the 18th and 19th centuries expand on the same theme.

    Many social scientists, following Marx, have analyzed power in terms of class. Seductive though this approach is, it seems to have been used as a means of ordering social, political, and economic events in a preconceived manner, thus oversimplifying the complex interactions of often a large set of power bases. Class analysis in housing was explored in "Housing, Rent and Regulation" (Lehrer 1980C), which discussed much of the writing on urban and housing problems done by Marxists (Beirne 1977, Saunders 1980, Harvey 1973, and Marcuse 1979). We have not repeated the same analysis here since it would have represented a substantial addition to the length of the study. Instead, class will be subsumed under other power bases, notably the economic/financial/material.

Finally, community power has been the subject of discussion in its own right by respected theorists (Ross 1967, Lappin 1967); but here too it is possible and therefore more economical to subsume community under polity and then, if appropriate, split the polity vertically into State, region, and local sub-region, as suggested elsewhere ("Power, Participation and the Regulation of Rent," Lehrer 1984).

CHAPTER 2

The Power Bases of Private Residential Landlords, Tenants, and Homeowners

Setting the Scene: An Overview of Actors and Power Components in the Organization of Housing

Property—in French, *la propriété*, meaning ownership and cleanliness, translates easily back into the English, propriety, that which is proper. How closely connected property ownership has been to the concept of what is right and proper. This is true to such a degree that property and rights have been linked not only by language and therefore social usage but also by law and political enfranchisement, e.g., in suffrage rights based on property ownership.

In this analysis the focus is not on personal but real property, as the legal fraternity would call it, and not on commercial, industrial, or agricultural realty but merely on residential real property. Who provides it, who uses it, who enjoys it, and who controls its provision, use, and enjoyment? Who maintains it, and to whose standards? Who controls its distribution? What changes can be seen in all the above activities, which can be regarded in many senses as power processes. What governs those changes, and how, if at all, do they link with other broader or analogous societal processes?

It is the contention of this study that a fruitful approach to answering such questions, which are mostly empirical, is by means of an analysis of power distribution and utilization. Here, with minor modifications for purposes of housing analysis, the taxonomy of power set out in figure 1 has been formalized in figure 2, with the addition of the principal actors in residential property listed in the first column. The purpose of figure 2 is to relate those power bases making up a major part of the aggregate of power in society to housing. Housing is the particular sub-system of society that this thesis is employing to illustrate the workings of power, including those less often dealt with in housing research. Further on in the chapter, the focus is narrowed to private sector rental housing, but at the outset, at least, it is intended to demonstrate the potential of relating all power bases to all the major housing actors.

7

This chapter is an attempt to relate some of the various components of power listed in the second column of figure 2 to some of those groups interacting in the provision, distribution, and organization of housing, which are listed in the first column. The activities of housing actors will thus be analysed in terms of their principal power bases, using figure 2 as a guiding framework. Since it is too wide a task to embrace all major actors in housing, the principal ones focused on will be those involved in private rental housing, namely residential landlords and tenants. However, homeowners will be used as a reference point in discussing possession and usage of power bases. As well, the role of government in the provision and distribution of housing will be introduced in terms of its power bases.

Figure 2:
Groups in Housing and Components of Power

Groups in Housing	Components of Power
Private Tenants	Religious/Moral/Ideological
Private Landlords	Coercive/Military
Homeowners & Hybrids	Spatial/Territorial
Construction Industry	Traditional/Patrimonial
Maintenance Trades	Political/Numerical
Real Estate Industry	Judicial/Quasi-Judicial
Property Management &	Legislative
Consulting Businesses	Public Administrative
Financial Institutions	Economic/Financial
Private Profit	Socio/Cultural
Private Non-profit	Organizational
Government & Agencies:	Personal/Socio/Psychological
Federal/Regional/Local	Informational/Technical/Media
Public Tenants	Decision-Making/Executive

The Economic Power Base of Landlords and Tenants

Of all the power bases, the landlord is expected to have a surfeit of power in base 9, i.e., in economic and financial power. It is axiomatic in "radical," pro-tenant literature that the landlord will be laden with superfluous wealth.[1] The basis of the assumption that landlords are economically more powerful than tenants appears to be that any person who owns property must ipso facto be wealthier than a person who does not. The argument that a person who does not own *residential* property may have a far higher disposable income, and therefore be able to indulge in a higher standard of living than a person with residential property, especially one with residential rental property who might be required to spend much of his income maintaining the property, will be treated at greater length in a later chapter. A few anecdotal examples based on Toronto apartments may nonetheless serve to provide some backdrop to the argument to be developed here.

- In the sauna of a downtown rental apartment building that the author frequents, two resident tenants were discussing a TV sale at a department store. The sale was of a high quality, rare console model, the price of which was marked down drastically from $16,000 to a little over $10,000. (1982 prices: a Ford Mustang was then $6-7,000.) It was considered a manifestly good value and was being considered for purchase by one of the tenants.

- In the same sauna, another tenant who had fitted out one of his two bedrooms into an audio-visual recording studio (when questioned on cost, a vague figure in the thousands was all that was offered) had decided to relinquish his apartment, which had been rent-controlled for eight years and therefore by his own admission one of the best bargains around, in order to purchase a pleasant two-bedroom condominium overlooking the lake in the Harbourfront complex (costing something in excess of $150,000).

- A perusal of the underground residential parking lot for one of the High Park buildings subject to the Cadillac-Fairview sale showed a generous sprinkling of vehicles costing over $30,000, including many Mercedes-Benz, Jaguars, and BMWs, as well as the usual Corvettes and some more exotic sports cars—(Alfas, Pumas, Lancias, etc.). Not one vehicle could have been classified as an old banger, the oldest being an impeccably maintained classic. Apart from a couple of boats being stored there, the rest of the parking area would have done credit to a well-kept, moderately expensive used car showroom. Noteworthy, also, is the relationship of the monthly lease costs of apartments in the complex ($250 to $500) to the monthly lease costs of the more exotic automobiles ($350 to $700). To the extent that some tenants had leased their cars rather than purchased them outright, they were spending more on the finance of their automobiles alone (ignoring the maintenance costs, etc.), than they had to pay in total for their accommodation.

- A cab driver, after grumbling about how his rent was due, confided that it only takes him two to three days' work to make up his monthly rent payment (10 percent rent-to-income ratio).

On the basis of this anecdotal evidence it is possible to argue that some tenants have a high level of disposable income relative to their housing costs, which they may expend on some luxurious commodities, foods, and services, albeit not on controlled rent, nor in most cases on residential real property.

The phenomenon is not, however, restricted to anecdotal evidence from Toronto. In Holland, another country governed by social democracy, half of the renting population were found to have been paying out less than 11 percent of their net incomes in rent. According to a survey quoted by the *London Financial Times*'s special feature on the Netherlands, "Squatters' protests highlight serious problem" (23 December 1980, 7),

> Many people have come to expect low rents and adjusted their spending accordingly. All accept that they will pay the market rate for their summer holiday or washing machine, but protest at every guildes in rent, said the building industry employers.

Popular Conception Erroneous

Some tenants, then, may be considered to have more economic power, in the sense of disposable cash, than do some non-corporate landlords, something quite contrary to the popular conception of poor tenants and rich landlords.

This can be nicely illustrated by a trip around Toronto's East End and Parkdale areas, where a large number of small landlords rent out units in duplexes and triplexes. No Mercedes or Jaguars in these parts, and very few shiny, late-model cars either. No glossy, fancy restaurants, and the homes look for the most part in need of a shine, if not something more drastic. In short, in low-income areas landlords exhibit no obvious greater wealth than their tenants, but many turn out to be the ones in shabbier dress, with shabbier possessions, which often includes their living units. For example, an old Polish couple off Queen Street rent out their large, two-bedroom, second floor, self-contained unit and live in a smaller unit on the ground floor, using a makeshift bathroom in the basement. They have lived this way for over thirty years, and their daughter advises that they raised a family of two downstairs, with the children giving a large portion of their incomes, when becoming employed, to the upkeep of the house. These are clearly live-in landlords. Likewise, a Polish widow living in a basement apartment off Queen Street has been renting the second and third floors as two self-contained apartments. She intends to sell her house in the next year in order to invite her sister from Poland to take a vacation to Hawaii for the first time—a life-long ambition. Similar histories abound among ethnic immigrants.

The anecdotal "eyewitness" evidence given above of many small (ethnic minority) landlords living quite modestly with little disposable income was given official corroboration by Toronto Housing Commissioner George Cook on 17 May 1983, as he gave evidence at a public meeting of Mayor Art Eggleton's Task Force on Ex-Psychiatric Patients. Reva Gerstein, appointed to head the Task Force, was then reported as greatly concerned about the lack or inadequacy of housing for the ex-patients. Based on a city survey of 10 rooming houses, the commissioner is reported as saying: "Most rooming-house owners operate on a shoestring budget and can't afford the renovations, no matter how badly needed they are" (*Toronto Star,* "Pay for fixing rooming houses, province told," 18 May 1983, A6).

This research by the city would thus cast doubt on the economic power of small landlords, dealing with low-income housing. Some of the responses of Ontario landlords answering a questionnaire likewise cast doubt on the wealth of all landlords and, conversely, the poverty of tenants (see appendix B).[2]

Why the Myth?

Why, then, the virtually undisputed myth of vast economic power belonging to landlords? Why is it invariably considered, not as a relative differential but as an absolute, that the landlords' monopoly of economic power is in direct contrast to the tenants' virtual economic powerlessness? Why have all landlords been lumped together, small and large, rich and poor, private and public, and tarred with the same brush? Evidence of the myth of their monolithic class image and economic power is provided in figures 3 through 7, showing quotes from newspaper articles and a selection of cartoons from three separate publications.

Figure 3:
Media Quotes from the *Toronto Star*

Thousands pay unlawfully high rent, probe told
"Thousands of Metro tenants are being charged unlawfully high rents, but there's only 'a rap on the knuckles' for landlords caught cheating, a provincial enquiry into rent control has been told."
[Suggesting the rapacity and immorality of landlords.]

Renters say controls don't protect against illegally high hikes
"...in spite of complaints, landlords are doing all right. One way this is shown, some tenants say, is that most landlords don't bother applying for increases beyond 6 percent. Operating profit isn't the main thing landlords look for, says tenant leader Dale Martin, but rather capital gains and tax benefits.
"Nazla Dane lives on Old Forest Hill Road, a snazzy part of town. Her building, she says, was put up in 1939, paid off long ago, and 'they've been creaming off profit for years.'"

Figure 3 continued

Jobless, widowed mom fears Saudi-Cadillac deal rent hikes

"The Cadillac-Fairview deal tops off the worst year in Carolyne Goar's life.

"The 29-year-old widow rents a townhouse for $428...one of 10,931 units in Metro sold to Saudi-Arabian investors recently.

"Now Goar fears that a hefty rent increase will leave Matthew, her 15 month-old-son, and herself without a home...

"The rumor circulating around the complex these days is that there will be a 60-per-cent rent hike to help finance the $500 million Saudi deal."

[No rent increase had been asked for at the time.]

Class politics make a comeback

"But most people today cannot afford to buy houses. They are going to have to raise kids and live out their lives in apartments with landlords trying to squeeze every nickel possible out of them...Landless tenants have become the new, large and permanent class in Toronto."

Greedy owners, vicious tenants, everyone's losing in Parkdale

"The Parkdale Problem: it began several years ago as a get-rich-quick scheme among landlords cheaply converting the area's once-stately homes into 'bachelorettes.'"

[Clayton Ruby, described in the article as] "a dynamic, high-profile civil rights lawyer" is quoted as saying: "What I'm doing is socially worthwhile and that makes me happy. It's not as good as a murder but I feel it's important for the city to find a method of stopping greedy landlords and protecting tenants."

84% of tenants, homeowners want rent controls, poll says

"Thousands of tenants in Metro and across the province in rent-controlled apartments are being hit with increases of more than double the 6 per cent...

"Applications for this year beginning April 1 are up nearly 40 per cent, with 3,130 landlords already having applied hikes for 94,878 apartment units...

"For Bill and Winnifred Bailey of Pacific Ave. it could be a serious blow to their pride and lifestyle.

"Bailey, who's retired, says he's now paying close to half of their income for their nearly $450-a-month high-rise apartment.

"Their landlord, giant Cadillac-Fairview Corp., is selling nearly 11,000 apartment units to Greymac Credit Corporation for $270 million."

Figure 4

The scheming, villainous landlord, wearing a top hat (a symbol of capitalism) in contrast to the honest and perplexed appearance of the tenant.

Source: R. McInnes, *Landlord/Tenant Rights in Ontario*, Self-Council Press: North Vancouver, 1980. Reproduced with permission.

Figure 5

Again, the top hat and Ebeneezer Scrooge clone appear, this time towering over supplicant, tearful tenants with baby in a slum apartment.

Source: B. Teall, *Tenant Hotline Handbook*, p. 10.

Figure 6

The landlord living it up on the backs of his tenants while pretending poverty.

Source: B. Teall, *Tenant Hotline Handbook*, p. 3.

Figure 7

The archetypical evil "super-capitalist pig," devoid of humanitarian qualities.

Source: "Tenants and the Law," joint publication of National Youth Council of New Zealand and New Zealand University Student's Association Auckland, 1978.

The reason landlords have been branded with negative stereotypes has little to do with contemporary economics. Historically there was a huge difference between the economic power of landlords and tenants. This would appear to have eroded, to the extent that income differentials have diminished. To the extent that the trend of incomes has gone upwards, measured in real terms, and the trend of residential rents has cumulatively declined, again measured in real terms, naturally the economic power base of landlords must have eroded, both relative to previous times and relative to tenants' economic power.[3]

The "nest-egg" approach is the alternative argument that can be raised to demonstrate the landlords' economic power versus the tenants' relative power-lessness. Again, historically this might have had substantial validity. However, the contemporary value of a landlord's "nest-egg," i.e., the capital value of his property, has been substantially reduced compared to the past and compared to general kinds of income, consumption, and wealth, which are reasonable indicators of economic power. In Ontario, this is based on the following four factors at work in Ontario: 1) shrinking real rents, 2) the close finan-cial/economic relationship between rent generation and capital value, 3) the Christmas 1982 Ontario "emergency" legislation that far more stringently restricted the capital cost pass-through in the calculation of admissible rent increases, which precipitated 4) an extremely constrained resale market in residential rental properties.

Territorial/Spatial Power of Landlords and Tenants

Territorial/spatial power is normally discussed under the heading of national sovereignty. It may be argued that whilst a people without any land base will be considered homeless, outcast, rootless, highly insecure, and therefore in many senses powerless, nonetheless territorial expansion brings with it the potential vulnerability to attack so great as to often negate the increased power that possession of increased territory might have been expected to produce.

At an individual level, territorial/spatial power is still seen as belonging to the landlord. It represents possibly one of the strongest reasons for small landlords entering into the business, and then staying in it in the face of an increasingly hostile environment. Both the landlord and the tenant may be expected to perceive the physical space to "belong" to the landlord. This sense of belonging may be strongest in the small-scale situation, where a home has been split into units and the landlord still lives in one of them. But this perception does not disappear entirely on the part of the tenants even in large, custom-built blocks where the owner is not resident or where ownership is held by a corporation. The landlord in the small, personal situation will perceive that his possession of the property gives him exclusive authority over how to use it. As a staff member from Toronto's Tenant Hotline (a municipally-funded, non-profit community organization) commented, it is becoming increasingly evident that landlords in the main, in priding themselves in their sense of territorial power and inviolability, do not know how few legal rights still remain for them.[4] Tenants likewise often do not know their rights, and merely accept the territorial sovereignty of the landlord. The tenant may also hold the landlord responsible because of ownership, while conversely feel no responsibility himself because he is not the owner. The tenant, therefore, may make less claim to spatial power, since he has no proprietary sense.

Much recent legislation has attempted to severely curtail the territorial/spatial power of the landlord through restricting the reasons for tenant eviction. This has varied in Canada from province to province, and from time to time. In Ontario, for example, under 1983 legislation tenancies may be terminated during a tenancy agreement for continued non-payment of rent, and at the end of the tenancy period for consistent late payment of rent, noisy behaviour, major renovations, and for habitation by the owner or a member or his close family. To the extent that tenants have been provided with security of tenure, the balance of territorial/spatial power has swung covertly in the tenants' favour. According to Alderman Dorothy Thomas in a March 1983 meeting entitled "Do You Pay Too Much Rent?" which discussed issues arising out of the Thom Commission, tenants and their legal representatives invariably win if they challenge the eviction notice of their landlord. For example, in a recent court judgement, the tenants were told that they did not have to move out of their apartment during renovations if they were prepared to put up with the inconvenience, despite legal notice having been given by the landlord. In almost all instances, according to the alderman, when tenants have challenged whether the renovations are of a sufficiently substantial nature to warrant eviction under Ontario's provincial legislation, the courts have held in favour of the tenants and disallowed the eviction notice. (The significance of such a statement by an alderman lies in the fact that as a local political representative she not only emphasized the tenants' growing powers of tenure but put herself on record as actively supporting that process, and as being prepared to continue to help any tenants fight eviction orders.)

Similarly, at the Tenant Hotline annual general meeting, several cases were cited in which tenant eviction notices were successfully squashed. One case in which the landlord was reclaiming a unit for his close family, was rejected after court challenge because the landlord had formally registered title of the property under a corporation, and as the tenant representative gleefully expostulated, corporations can't have kids! (He meant of course that the court had ruled the landlord had to be human rather than a corporate body in order to successfully terminate a tenancy agreement on the grounds of needing a unit for himself or close family.)

One might therefore be witnessing the trend, anticipated by Macpherson (1978), away from rights of property ownership in housing, entrenched though they have been for centuries, to legal rights of quiet enjoyment, based on occupation and use of a property, and regardless of ownership. The "sitting tenant" phenomenon in the United Kingdom may be used to illustrate this. Until recently, the territorial/spatial power was taken for granted by landlords as a perquisite of property ownership and accepted by tenants for socio-psychological reasons. To the extent that it has been challenged by tenants and their representatives with recourse to political, legal, and judicial power bases, and under conditions of conflict, it has proven increasingly weak. Spatial/territorial power may now be confined to informal use by individual landlords in conjunction with their other power bases, such as organizational and socio-psychological.

Organizational and Executive/Decision-Making Power

Increased territorial power (as in larger numbers of holdings of rental units) may then be substantially dependent on increased organizational power at micro- as well as macro-levels of society, e.g., at the level of individual enterprises and at the level of regional and federal governments. Organizational, executive, and decision-making power at the individual landlord-tenant level may still be expected to favour the landlord: he is, after all, in the driver's seat, able to make the rules, and determine to whom he will rent and which criteria to use in choosing tenants. He may also decide when and to what level of quality he will maintain different buildings and, indeed, different units in the same building. Prior to special landlord-tenant legislation, a landlord's organizational power was largely uncircumscribed in terms of choosing tenants, setting rents, establishing maintenance policies and housekeeping routines, and effecting evictions. This gave him decided organizational and executive/decision-making power advantages over tenants.

But now, in most Western democracies only narrow limits are left to the total discretion of the landlord in any of these areas. His decision-making/executive power is still essential to keep the rental organization functioning, but it is constrained in all areas by legislation, which varies in scope and stringency from country to country and in Canada from province to province. But in all cases it tends to change the emphasis from landlord organizational and executive *power* to a landlord's organizational and executive *responsibility*.

By contrast, it would appear that at a group level of landlord-tenant relations the organizational power of tenants has increased in recent years. In an article headed "Tenants feisty in '82," the popular Toronto weekly *Now* (23 December 1982 to 5 January 1983, p. 5) stated:

> 1982 may be the year tenant power coalesced in Ontario...The Federation of Metro Tenants Associations has grown 250 percent in a few months, and now represents tenants in 25,000 units, according to organizer Leslie Robinson.

Even local area newspapers in Toronto found the growing trend of tenant organizing sufficiently newsworthy to give it front page headline coverage. For example *The Villager*, a West Toronto newspaper, carried the headline, "Tenants organizing to fight multiple ownership threat" (15 June 1983, p. 1). A U.S. housing publication *Shelterforce* went one stage further: under a large caption "Tenant Power" they ran the article "The Tenant Vote: How Groups Use Elections to Win Political Power,"which explained how tenants' associations could and should use "elections as an organizing tool," stating that,

Much organizing has been done, rent strikes, demonstrations, media campaigns have been used with success. Tenants must continue this kind of direct action and organizing... Although tenants are only one third of the American population, in most cities they are a majority, and often a substantial one. There is no reason why tenants cannot become an effective voting bloc in most major cities. It's a question of organization and will... In cities across the country, tenants' groups have become involved in elections. The most common way this takes place is in pushing legislation... The results in Santa Monica, for example, show that the tenants' movement can both elect its own people to public office and focus on basic issues like rent control... (*Shelterforce*, vol. 6, no. 2, May 1981, 6-7).

Socio-Psychological Power

Closely connected with the degree of balance or imbalance of spatial/territorial and organizational power is the social-psychology of power relations between individual landlords and tenants. This deals not with the legalities and economics of power but with each party's perceptions of its power, and that of the other. For example, a landlord's unchallenged territorial power in former times gave him a huge psychological advantage over his tenants, which one may assume continues to colour both a tenant's and a landlord's "social construction of reality" (Berger & Luckman 1966), despite plenty of concrete evidence to the contrary. Guarantees exist in law to protect the tenant's privacy and security. In Ontario, for instance, the private landlord cannot enter units, except in cases of emergency, without 24 hours' notice in writing, and only at reasonable times. He cannot raise rent without three months' written notice in acceptable legal form, and then only once a year and for a maximum permitted under the "rent review" legislation—currently in the 4 percent range—unless a higher amount is authorized by the quasi-judicial body after a process that currently takes years to complete. Nor can he evict summarily, change locks, charge security deposits, or keep tenants' personal property until past rent is paid, etc. Yet despite these and more protective measures, many tenants might well remain intimidated by the legacy of a past when landlords did indeed have relatively unfettered territorial rights, and therefore exploitable interpersonal power.

Perhaps one can explain this social-psychological legacy in Goffman's (1959) terms. For centuries landlords have had a virtual monopoly, not so much in economic terms of cash income, but in the dramaturgical terms of setting the stage, dictating the situation, and setting the terms in which the landlord-tenant play will be acted. It is true, to extend Goffman's terminology further, that both sets of players maintain a backstage and a front stage, or a private and a public place for social exchange, but in former days the landlord was able to completely dominate the front stage, and, of greater psychological impact, he was *also able* to invade a tenant's backstage, so that little private space remained for the tenant's self-respect, or in Goffman's terms, for his individual cover. The landlord, on the other hand, had his backstage nicely protected and could therefore sustain as many roles as other circumstances permitted. Even now, the landlord literally holds the key to a tenant's living space, while the tenant has no reciprocal symbol of physical control. (The possession of keys, i.e., the control of access would represent an obvious manifestation of landlord spatial/territorial power. The extent to which he may use it has been drastically curtailed by access-restriction legislation. The conditions under which he might decide to use it would obviously vary from individual to individual.)

As in many other social situations, the legal realities of a situation may not coincide with social realities or the social/psychological perceptions of each party. To the extent that either party is embedded in different patterns of social perception (usually patterns reinforced by childhood memories or even intergenerational tradition), it may take much time or significant ruptures of previous practice to permanently change the social-psychological balance of power. This would appear to be valid in the area of landlord-tenant social relations.

A landlord's organizational power may serve to reinforce his social-psychological advantage. This is the "how" element of the power base, and it may be manifested in two ways. Within a fairly broad range, the landlord may decide when to fix, maintain, and renew the inside of a unit (appliances, washroom facilities, paintwork, floors, etc.) as well as the outside of a building. This puts the tenant de facto, if not de jure, into a dependent relation. Relating to Emerson's (1970) power-dependency relations analysis, the tenant can decide to depend less on the landlord by arranging to fix things himself. Emerson's approach implies that these so-called balancing operations are the norms.

It is here suggested that there is no norm for balancing operations, or for the conditions in which a landlord will utilize his organizational power in favour of or in detriment to the tenant. Each situation may become more *or less* balanced. In the specific context of landlord-tenant relations one has to differentiate between individual relations and group relations. In the latter, there has been a marked shift in the balance of power. In the former, there may be some wash-effect spilling over from the groups' changing power balance, but one must be cautious not to assume wide-sweeping and universal changes at the individual level.

The imposition of "organizational dependency," then, is one way that landlords have traditionally built up and reinforced their social-psychological power. The other is purely by office, position, or official status (see French and Raven's "positional power," 1969). A one-man renting operation may have precious little of this type of organizational power because he cannot avoid personal face-to-face relations or submerge behind a bureaucratic facade, while the accountant or bookkeeper of a 10-man operation may be more successful in intimidating a tenant into, for example, supplying 12 post-dated rent cheques or paying a penalty for late rent. (Both, by the way, are unenforceable by law in Ontario. See R. McInnes, *Landlord/Tenant Rights in Ontario*, 1980, p. 29.) The ability to set the rules and procedures to determine when and how things are done, and to dominate the front stage with a more or less convincing and comprehensive bureaucratic act, can be expected to serve the landlord in dominating the tenant in his establishment of social relations. He may then be in a position to determine the framework for the psychological perceptions of their relative power differentials.[5]

How severely tenants have in fact felt trapped, helpless, and intimidated by landlord oppression must depend on the time, place, socio-economic status of the landlord relative to them, their ability to find alternative accommodation (reducing objective dependency in Emerson's terminology), as well as the degree of their own perceptions of oppression and helplessness. What is being stressed here is the significance of the tenants' mind-set, while not rejecting the possibility and utility of empirically validating the more manifest aspects contributing to tenants' social-psychological power. The manifest and to some extent measurable aspects, such as class, race, ethnic background, socio-economic status, etc., have been addressed in empirical studies carried out mostly in the United States (Sternlieb 1972, Sternlieb & Hughes 1976). A similar type of mind-set analysis of socio-psychological power is equally valid when applied to landlords.

Homeowners' Non-Economically Based Power, Relative to Tenants, Landlords, and Levels of Government

Homeowners constitute a major actor in the organization of housing. They also act as a useful basis of comparison to tenants as consumers of housing and to landlords as suppliers of housing.

Principally because of the nature of their economic power base, namely their investment, homeowners can be thought of as having more power than tenants in some contexts and less in others. They are normally considered more autonomous, they are not beholden to a landlord for the use of their residence, and they can expect to have unfettered enjoyment of occupation. Yet all their enjoyments and rights of ownership are quite circumscribed. Those homeowners with mortgages are obliged to make regular payments to mortgage holders, with possibly less chance of sufferance and latitude than in the case of tenants paying rent.[6] They are constrained by neighbours' rights from complaining to municipal authorities about noise, uncut grass, unswept leaves, unshovelled snow, and generally unkempt appearances. The whole slew of inspectors who can plague a landlord (hydro, building, health, etc.), can equally enforce the letter of the by-law against a homeowner. However, a homeowner may find fewer complaints lodged against him than his landlord counterpart.

With regard to their numerical power in the political context, and their organizational power, homeowners score high in the former and low in the latter. Insofar as they constitute a large proportion of the voting population and can perceive a common group interest, they should be able to wield considerable political power. But homeowners have not, historically, often organized themselves as a common interest or pressure group. This is not to say that homeowners' or ratepayers' associations do not exist, but their activities have been concerned with highly local matters, such as road widening, sewerage construction, and their effects on specific neighbourhoods and roads. The associations have tended to be issue-focused, strengthening their organizational structure and cohesion temporarily in order to deal with a particular issue, and sinking into a dormant state after its resolution. A good illustration of this phenomenon, which received wide publicity during the 1983 Metro Toronto municipal elections, was the issue of the proposed Glen Manor half-way house to be set up in a somewhat exclusive residential Beaches area in Toronto. The property owners' association even demonstrated sufficient communal economic power to raise among its members enough money to outbid the purchase offer of the group proposing a half-way home. The alderman candidates, of course, were forced to make statements and take stands on the issue, it being fortuitously the peak period of the municipal election campaign. The young, inexperienced candidate of 22 years of age, who had been most out-spoken on behalf of the property owners association in the much publicized half-way house issue, found himself unexpectedly receiving enough votes to be elected as senior alderman for the Beaches area.

Homeowners, then, may band together around an issue of common interest if they feel their adversary is worth the bother of taking on, and they have a reasonable chance of winning. Banks and other monolithic financial institutions with apparently unassailable economic power may not seem worth that bother, since the result of the struggle would be a foregone conclusion. Otherwise, homeowners' power remains more or less as dormant as their profile, but not forgotten by canny politicians who must remain conscious of voters to maintain their representational political power or, to put it more plainly, to stay most securely in office. This awareness explains the relief subsidy systems quickly announced by federal Finance Minister Allen McEachen's ill-fated 1981 budget statement, which was meant to forestall or at least palliate any ground swell of revolt by homeowners when their mortgage interest rates soared. Relief was only to be given, however, to those in "dire straits," as the government called homeowners in imminent danger of losing their homes. Therefore, during this period the majority of homeowners searching for mortgage financing were forced to accept the historically unprecedented interest rates quoted at 20 percent and more. The *Toronto Star* reported that Prime Minister Trudeau "confirmed that homeowners should not look to the federal government for help in renegotiating their mortgages" (16 May 1981, A1). As a more or less unorganized constituency, their numerical power was manifestly presumed not to be easily converted into substantial political power. Despite a common interest rate problem, however, homeowners did not organize in sufficient strength to radically affect government policy in their favour.[7]

Similarities and Differences

In analysing their respective power bases one may come to see that homeowners and tenants share some common properties. They are both highly numerous, and until recently, both have been quite unorganized and not very conscious of the potential political power of their members. To the extent that either group has organized, it has tended to be to deal with a particular issue. The most recent one for tenants has been the previously cited issue of the 1982 wholesale attempted sale and re-sale of some 11,000 apartment units in Metro Toronto. But although both groups appear to need issues to arouse them from dormancy and to galvanize them into some level of organized activity, tenants have a few advantages that homeowners do not possess:

- They have a ready-made and highly visible adversary, the landlord, to act as an on-going focal point. As discussed in the previous chapter, power is highly relational and while tenants are automatically locked into a conflict relationship with landlords, homeowners have no such on-going potential adversary group to pit their strength and energy against (lending organizations, developers, municipal inspectors, and property tax authorities provide some adversarial grist for a homeowner's power mill, but not on a similar on-going basis as do landlords for tenants).

- Issues that are common to all tenants appear more frequently than issues that involve all homeowners. For example, in Ontario the 1970 Landlord Tenant Act, the 1975 Rent Control Act, subsequent rent review amending legislations, and most recently, the Thom Commission have each affected virtually all private residential tenants. By contrast, even the interest rate "crisis" (a terribly over-used word, as is argued in the final chapter, but still the one used by most financial analysts in describing interest rate increases in 1981), only affected the small minority of homeowners who were compelled to seek re-financing during that period. Even then, it only affected them to the extent that they were unable or unwilling to pay off all or part of existing mortgages.

- Tenants have constantly been reminded of their political power, in Ontario at least, by the overt wooing of their votes by the majority of politicians, no matter what colour. For example, during the Cadillac-Fairview sale, headlines in the *Toronto Star* declared "Tenants to be protected, Elgie says" (16 November 1982, A1), and "MPPs demand halt to apartment deal" (16 November 1982, A11). (See also, for example, the Ontario Liberal Party brochure, entitled "Tenant News," with headlines like "Have you been paying too much rent?" and the declaration of a "Tenants' Bill of Rights" [spring 1983]. See also appendix C for a synopsis of the three major political parties' responses to a *Globe and Mail* questionnaire relating among other issues to rent controls. Similar "bills of rights" have yet to be produced by the political parties for homeowners or landlords.)

- The consciousness of tenants' common interests, their organizing power, and their potential political and economic power as a group has been deliberately raised by full-time, permanent tenant organizers who have been funded by the provincial government and city hall; and likewise, by the tenant-help activities of the publicly funded legal aid clinics, all except one of which have refused to help abused landlords on the basis of conflict of interest.[8]

- The founding and impressive growth record (250 percent in 1982) of an umbrella organization for tenant groups, the Federation of Metro Tenant Associations, represents their interests, radicalizes members through organizing rent protest meetings and disseminating rent freeze literature for as many tenants as possible, and provides useful media coverage through links with the press. Concrete evidence of the extent of their political and economic power was manifested by their ability during the Cadillac-Fairview re-sale to impose sufficient pressure on the provincial government to have the re-sale investigated by a Royal Commission, and to have new legislation hastily introduced to restrict rent increases to 5 percent as a result of re-financing charges.

All five factors listed above have contributed to the politicization and consciousness raising of the power of tenants as a group, with no corresponding set of activities at work for homeowners as a group. This should not be construed to mean that tenants ipso facto have more power than homeowners.

The five factors merely help explain the facility of tenants to organize, which homeowners have not shown.

Landlords, likewise, have had no parallel set of mutually-reinforcing, government-encouraged and government-funded factors to galvanize them into a more potent cohesive power group. (This is true despite the Multiple Dwelling Standards Association's activities and, in particular, the virtually single-handed efforts of its president, Jan Schwartz, by now a recognized spokesman for middle-range landlords in Ontario.) Conflict and a visible common adversary in housing have therefore increased the organizational power base of some housing actors, notably that of the tenant (in some respects analogous to unions and the growth of countervailing organizational power, as described by Galbraith, 1970).[9]

Power Bases

Figure 8 is an attempt to summarize the principal power bases on which each major actor in housing is seen to rely, and the main actors with which each major actor interacts and interdepends. In some ways summaries such as these can be misleading, insofar as they do not attach weights to the strengths of power bases possessed and used by each actor. For example, it is suggested that both private tenants and private landlords have some economic power, but that the tenants' power is easily ignored or underestimated, while the landlords' may be severely overestimated, intentionally or otherwise. Similarly, the number of power bases on which an actor can draw does not necessarily accurately reflect his aggregate power. An actor may have such a large quantum of power in say, three bases, that he or she totally outweighs another whose aggregate power is spread over many more bases. Moreover, borrowing again from Galbraith's theory of countervailing power, an actor who perceives himself or herself in the fortunate position of not being threatened, may not consider it necessary to amass a great deal of power. For example, in figure 8 one sees that homeowners do not appear to have acquired a great arsenal of power bases. In providing a summary of power and inter-relationships to date, figure 8 may be considered useful in setting the scene for a more dynamic analysis of those elements in housing that are changing. The small degree of power gathering by some housing actors may be best explained by their perception that they are relatively secure and autonomous already, so that accumulation of additional power bases would be superfluous. This is borne out by inspection of the relatively few main interdependencies outlined for homeowners and, perhaps more, by the relatively unthreatening nature of these interdependencies. Contrast this with the situation of private landlords and tenants. Here there are possibly more power bases at the ready, but the number of interdependencies and the level of threat each represents to the actor are quite different than for homeowners.

Figure 8
Main Power Bases and Interdependencies of Actors in Housing

MAIN POWER BASES

Private Tenants	Private Landlords	Homeowners
Ideological	Spatial/Territorial	Ideological
Political/Numerical	Traditional	Spatial/Territorial
Legislative	Economic/Financial	Political/Numerical
Public Administrative	Organizational	Legislative
Economic/Financial	Personal/	Socio-Cultural
Socio-Cultural	Socio-Psychological	Economic/Financial
Media	Decision-Making/	
	Executive	

MAIN INTERDEPENDENCIES

Private Tenants	Private Landlords	Homeowners
Private landlords	Private tenants	Maintenance trades
Government agencies	Government agencies	Real estate industry
including the judiciary	(same as tenants)	Property mgmt. &
Quasi judicial admin.	Media	consulting businesses
bodies dealing with	Construction industy	Financial institutions
landlord-tenant relations	Maintenance trades	Public Tenants (in some
Building maintenance	Real estate industry	situations)
control agencies	Property mgmt. &	
Legislative bodies	consulting businesses	
Media	Financial institutions	

Notes

1. The following extracts from *No Place Like Home—Britain's Housing Tragedy* by Frank Allaun, MP (1972) may help illustrate:
    Ch. 8: Rachman Road
    This is one of the worst streets in the district. The four-storey tenements are over a hundred years old, all owned by two landlords, who are estimated to be making 7,500 pounds a year, clear, out of the properties...These dwellings contain almost every housing defect: damp, vermin, overcrowding, lack of lavatories and bathrooms, rotting walls and ceilings, faulty drains. Yet many of the tenants here somehow managed to keep their homes clean and decent. (p. 112.)
    Message: Rich, greedy, uncaring landlords trod down decent, clean tenants. Note that "Rachman Road" is a foreign (Jewish Rumanian) pseudonym given to the road to depict the type of landlord. Rachman lent his name to a new word in the English language: "Rachmanism," phenomenon of "foreign" (ethnic minority) slum landlording.
    Ch. 9: MP Against the Landlords
    Arthur Lathan M.P.:
    "There are some cases of appalling landlords who deliberately neglect the dwellings for which they are responsible. Even those where the landlords are relatively 'good' the living conditions are far from any reasonable standard...We have a number of cases where the landlord, having collected maybe $1500 a year rent from a single multi-occupied property...without spending on repairs, and then sells the property, he can recoup his original outlay with a pretty substantial margin remaining." (p. 123.)

2. It might be considered more appropriate to distinguish between small landlords and rooming house owners. Two comments are apposite: rooming house owners can reasonably be considered a category of small landlords, rather than a different species; and from the Metro report it appears that rooming house owners are a breed dying faster than other categories of landlords, so that it would seem empirically more practical to lump them in with other small landlords, thus maintaining a more substantial aggregate population base for study.

3. This is not to argue that the mean income of tenants as a whole is higher than the mean income of landlords as a whole. However, it does underline that increasing numbers of relatively well-off salaried urbanites find it economically advantageous to remain as tenants, thus preventing landlords from reaping maximum financial gain, and thus further changing the balance of relative economic power.

4. The staff person was representing his organization in an address to a tenants' public meeting held in downtown Toronto to assert tenants' rights in the face of impending new legislation.

5. Should all this sound too much like a Kafka nightmare and more than a Goffman-like analysis, it is in fact to Kafka to whom we must turn for vivid illustrations and brilliant insights into the humiliations and frustrations felt by victims of organizational conspiracy. His is the gift of conveying the subtle and manifold minutiae of feelings of dependency and neuroses of eroding self-worth, which a human being deprived of all normal power bases may undergo. (Kafka 1963.)

6. A feature article in the *Globe and Mail* (25 March 1982, 10) describes how many homeowners in areas like Windsor, Sudbury, and other smaller towns in southern Ontario are abandoning their homes and vandalizing them when they find themselves unable to meet increased mortgage payments. It is noteworthy that the sense of economic impotence leads so quickly and apparently inevitably to a diffuse sense of powerlessness, then to frustration and alienation, and finally to a manifest rejection of the responsibilities of ownership through acts of vandalism. To quote the article:

> Telefern spokesman Elain Behnke says vandalism is becoming increasingly common: "You can see that people are really bitter about leaving their homes…Many simply abandon houses without notifying the mortgage company…They take the keys, turn off the heat or let the heating oil run out and leave the pipes to freeze and burst…"

Noteworthy too is the financial institution cited for enforcing repossession. It is not one of the major banks, but the local credit union, whose limited economic power and therefore whose discretion to conduct its affairs in a humane fashion, as discussed earlier, is highly circumscribed. To quote the article again:

> For weeks Michael Howe played hide-and-seek with his credit union manager, but last July his luck ran out. "He said he wanted to see me in his office," and the 25-year-old Inco miner and father of two already knew the reason: it was a week before his mortgage came due…Mr. Howe had been paying…10½ percent [for his mortgage]. The new rate was 21 percent. "We figured we'd have $7 left over before groceries."…Reluctantly, bitterly… they took the keys to their home to the credit union, and moved into an apartment.

7. How then, does one explain the capital grants offered by both federal and provincial governments to first-time home buyers and to purchasers of new homes? Not by homeowners' power, (though possibly by politicians' awareness of their potential powers), but by 1) a housing policy resulting from the near-zero vacancy rental market (due to rent controls) in order to encourage better-off renters to give up their units

and purchase homes; and 2) an economic policy that wanted to favour two organized groups of actors on the housing scene who considered themselves and economically appeared to be in extremely weak positions: the construction industry and the real estate industry. Both sets of grants helped the real estate industry in their sales activities and, therefore, won a few political brownie points in that constituency; but because of their relative lack of power, this was not a central aspect of the policy. The grants for new homes provided some impetus to new home demand so that the construction industry could off-load old inventory and start building new units, thus providing much-needed jobs in all the associated trades.

The grants for first-time home buyers of used homes had a more indirect and questionable economic effect. It may have been, in part, a covert way of avoiding a too unmanageable ground swell of resentment among the presently unorganized existing homeowners, as it gave them a better chance to off-load their cost-increased homes at a $3,000 discount paid for by the government (not in itself a sufficient sum of money in 1981 for a down payment on most properties in, for example, Toronto).

A third organized group that was helped by the grants was the financial institution: banks, mortgage and trust companies, mortgage brokers, and other smaller lending and associated organizations. These were all flushed with funds by virtue of savers rushing to take advantage of unprecedently high "investor" interest rates being offered to them along with a concomitant lack of demand for funds at such high rates. The effective discounting of residential properties by the two levels of government helped to re-flate the sagging demand for funds by homeowner borrowers. It was thus seen to help, and so partly mollified another set of organizational actors concerned with housing.

All three sets of actors then were perceived as having some political power by both federal and provincial levels of government, and, therefore, each was given some benefits by the introduction of an ad hoc new housing policy, namely the new grants announced at the conjunction of the economic and interest rate "crisis" with the housing slump in 1981.

8. This was mentioned by the Riverdale legal aid spokesman at a public meeting to discuss implications of the Thom Commission. He disagreed with the policy and said he was willing to help landlords, but despite his "open" policy, his clinic only helped landlords in 2 percent of cases.

9. Explanations of how, the extent to which, and the conditions under which various power resources are utilized by the different housing actors under discussion have been addressed in appropriate spots in the chapter. An additional note on these issues may still be considered useful. In general terms, the conditions under which power bases are utilized can often be

related to conflict or potential conflict situations. In the context of private rental housing, such a general condition would be created by, for example, a low vacancy rate. Specific circumstances that could be expected to generate conflict situations would be such events as the sale of an apartment building, which would pose a threat to the security and/or low rent levels of the existing tenants. The publicizing of such potential threats will often precipitate a conflict situation and from there a "power struggle." The role of the media can be significant in generating and manipulating the conditions under which power resources are marshalled in such conflict situations as the beginning of this chapter showed. See also the bibliography of newspaper articles for more examples.

CHAPTER 3

The Power of the Individual Small Landlord

Introduction

Much has been and continues to be written in the popular press and in academic texts in the United Kingdom, Canada, and the United States on the frustrations, deprivations, and degradations experienced by tenants at the hands of landlords, the tenants' consequent or perhaps concomitant sense of powerlessness in the face of such situations, and their need to redress the situation by such means as security of tenure coupled with rent controls.[1]

Much of the emphasis in these writings has been on the difficulties encountered by the (financially) poor tenant. The implication has been that many if not the majority of tenants are poor and underprivileged, while the landlord can be assumed a priori to be wealthy and "over-privileged." Yet very little empirical research has been undertaken with regard to the actual status, in economic, social, ethnic, or other terms, of the landlord population (Thernstrom 1973, Miron and Cullingworth 1983). In particular, since the largest number of landlords are "small landlords" (Greber 1952, Sternlieb 1966), i.e., those who own a small number of units (to be defined more rigorously below), there appears a need to address the identity and the power bases of these small private residential landlords as a specific group.

In this chapter two sources are primarily relied on to present the perceptions the small landlord may have of his situation vis-a-vis his tenants. The first source is Emily Carr's autobiographical account of her experiences as a landlady over a couple of decades in Victoria, B.C. The second source is based on a series of open interviews conducted with ten small landlords in Toronto. At the end of the chapter, a brief review is given of a small questionnaire survey of residential landlords in Ontario, which may help illustrate some of the points made through the previous two sources.

Emily Carr's Experiences of Small Landlording:
A Review of *The House of All Sorts*, 1944

In this autobiography, Emily Carr deals with the spatial/territorial power that is normally assumed to belong to the landlord and provides a very different perception of her sense of territorial power, one which is not encountered in landlord-tenant studies, but which is common among landlords. She writes,

As I approached my house from the street its grim outline seemed to slap me in the face. It was mine. Yet by paying rent, others were entitled to share it and to make certain demands upon me and upon my things. (p.79.)

The whole house, my flat, even my own studio, was more or less public. People could track me down in any part of the house or even in the garden. (p. 9.)

From the moment key and rent exchanged hands a subtle change took place in the attitude of renter towards owner.

The tenant was obviously anxious to get you out, once the flat was her's.... When once they had paid and called it "my flat" they were always asking for this or that additional furniture or privilege. (p. 19.)

Later, when Carr graciously offers some of her own space to accommodate guests of one of her tenants for a wedding visit, she notes:

The old lady was delighted...The girl would be two days with her parents before the ceremony. She was to have my spare room. However, the young man came too, so she had the couch in her mother's sitting room. They sent him upstairs [to Carr's flat] without so much as asking if they might. (pp. 26-27.)

Further on:

Every night between twelve and two the lawyer son came home to the flat. First he slammed the gate, then took the steps at a noisy run, opened and shut the heavy front door with such a bang that the noise reverberated throughout the whole still house...People complained. I went to the young man's mother and asked that she beg the young man to come in quietly. She replied, "My son is my son! We pay rent! Good day."

He kept on banging the house awake at two A.M. One morning at three A.M. my telephone rang furiously. In alarm I jumped from my bed and ran to it. A great Yawn was on the other end of the wire. When the yawn was spent, the voice of the lawyer's mother drawled, "My son informs me your housedog is snoring; kindly wake the dog, it disturbs my son"...I wanted to loose the Bobtails, follow them—run, and run, and run into forever—beyond the

sound of every tenant in the world—tenants tore me to shreds.
(p. 54.)

Powerlessness

The above quotations, and there are many more of the same ilk, do not represent the feelings of a person with a strong sense of territorial power, of rights grounded in her ownership and possession of property. On the contrary, the impression is given throughout her autobiography that Emily Carr felt like a prisoner to her property, an individual who by reason of her "landlord" role had lost all claim to privacy or "backstage" (Goffman 1959), and who was enslaved by tenants who could tyrannize her at will by reason of *their economic power over her*. A few quotations with respect to the economic "power" she felt she possessed by being owner of the property should illustrate:

I had expected to occupy the Studio flat and paint there, but now the House of All Sorts could not afford a janitor. I had to be everything. Rents had lowered, taxes risen. I was barely able to scrape a living...(p. 6.)

I had removed myself to a tent in the garden and a gas-ring in the basement for the summer months, ends being difficult to make meet. (p. 84.)

The purpose had been to provide a place in which I could paint and an income for me to live on. Neither objective was ever fully realized in the House of All Sorts. (p. 87.)

I asked her for the rent several times but she always put me off. Finally she said rudely, "I am not going to pay; my husband can."

I went to the man, who was most insolent, saying "My wife took the flat; let her pay."

"Come," I said "Time is going on, one or the other of you must pay." I pointed to the notice on the kitchen door "RENTS IN ADVANCE." He laughed in my face. "Bosh!" he said. "We don't pay till we're ready."

I began to make enquiries about the couple...Their record was shocking. They had rented from a war widow, destroyed her place, and gone off owing her a lot of money.

Both of the Panquists (the tenants in question) had jobs; they could pay...(pp. 34-34.)

And finally:

I hate pianos, tenants' pianos. They can make a landlady suffer so hideously...

Prospective tenants said, "You have no objection to a piano, of course."

"Oh, no," one lied, because one was *dependent* on tenants to pay mortgages and taxes. (p. 104, emphasis added.)

The Servant

Coupled with the economic impotence and dependence that Carr felt were several other themes that other part-time landlords later expressed in their comments, and that also arise elsewhere in this report: the usurpation of the landlord role over other, more significant aspects of life's work (in Emily Carr's case, her art); the necessity to be a jack-of-all-trades and to never attain specialized competence in any; the low social status attached to being a landlord, especially at the face-to-face level, and that is translated into low socio-psychological or personal power and low self-esteem in many cases; and a strong sense of alienation from one's power, one's clients, any status-conscious family members, and ultimately, of course, oneself (Marx 1964, 1972; Fox 1984). The following quotes will serve to illustrate:

I never painted if anyone was around and always kept my canvases carefully shrouded in dust sheets. I never did paint much in that fine studio that I had built; what with the furnace, tenants, cleaning and the garden there was no time. (p. 89.)

[The problem of having no time for oneself will be raised again in the mini-survey of Toronto small landlords later in the chapter.]

I wished my pictures did not have to face the insulting eyes of my tenants. It made me squirm. The pictures themselves squirmed me in their own right too. They were always whispering, "Quit, quit this; come back to your own job!" But I couldn't quit; I had this house and I had no money... (p. 89.)

My sisters, who lived round the corner from the House of All Sorts, watched my landladying with disapproval, always siding with the tenant...But they did not have to be landladies. (p. 21.)

The episode of Carr helping with a tenant's wedding is referred to bitterly once again, nicely illustrating the pariah status attaching to landladies:

I was helping Mrs. Pendergast finish the washing-up when the young couple arrived. Mrs. Pendergast went to the door. She did not bring them out where I was, but, keeping her daughter in the other room, she called out some orders to me as if I had been her servant. I finished and went away; I began to see that the old lady was a snob. She did not think me the equal of her daughter because I was a landlady. (p. 27.)

And, later, with a different tenant:

I had known the other bride since she was a child. When I welcomed her into my house, she chilled as if to remind me that she was a popular young bride—I a landlady; I took the hint...

When I asked her to hand back what she did not want, so that I might store them safely, she was very insulting, as if my things were beyond contempt or hurting. (p. 41.)

On Sunday morning the house was usually quiet. At seven A.M. my bell pealed violently. I stuck my head out into the drizzling rain and called, "What is wanted?"

Grannie's [an elderly tenant's] voice squeaked—"you!"

"Anything special? I am not up."

"Right away! Important!"

I hurried. Anything might have happened…When I opened the door, Grannie poked an empty vase at me, "The flowers you put in our flat are dead. More!" (p. 59.)

We were having one of our bitterest cold snows. I, as landlady, had just two jobs—shovelling snow—shovelling coal. (p. 70.)

Low Status

The feeling of alienation, of being a lackey, and of objectified labour (Marx 1964) in the above two quotes is obvious. Likewise, the sense of social stigma and low (inverted?) class/status is illustrated in the following quotation:

"Your rent was up five days ago, Mrs. Pillcrest." Taut with fury [the tenant replied] "Business! Kindly remember, Landlady, Mr. Pillcrest and I do not belong to that class." (p. 82-83.)

The act of tenants leaving the premises in a filthy state when they vacate is perhaps a fitting final parting gesture of contempt and hate, and will be bitterly referred to by the Toronto small landlords. It finds its way into Carr's autobiographical account too:

There was no sound from Lower East. All day blinds remained close drawn. The gas man came, asking that I let him into that silence to read the meter.

"The flat is still occupied, far as I know."

"Your tenant ordered his final reading this morning."

I took a pass key and went down. The place was in wild disorder, there were dozens of liquor bottles. In an attempt to be funny, they had been arranged ridiculously as ornaments. Things were soiled with spilled liquor. The place smelled disgusting. The bedding was stripped from the bed. The laundry man returned it later and told me it had been soaked with blood. My carving knife belonging to the flat was missing. (p. 98.)

And with a different set of tenants:

The woman left in a cab with a couple of suitcases…to describe the cleaning of that flat would be impossible. As a parting niceness the woman hurled a pot of soup—meat, vegetables and grease—down the kitchen sink. She said, "You hurried our moving," and shrugged. The soup required a plumber. (p. 15.)

At the time Emily Carr was a landlady, the law was far more strongly in favour of the landlord than it is today. Thus, she was able to informally give tenants minimum notice to vacate if they refused to pay the rent, etc. In Emily Carr's case (others were less fortunate, as seen below) she was able to have the local constable supervise the eviction of a tenant for non-payment of rent when she expressed fear of the tenant's reprisals. She was also able to distrain on tenants' personal possessions for partial reimbursement of unpaid rent. Nowadays evictions must go through due process of law, and the tenant has rights of appeal during which his tenure is protected. Distraining has been a criminal offence in Ontario since the early 1970s.

Unreliability

Despite the relatively supportive framework of legislation and judicial procedures under which Carr operated, it was still, according to her accounts, unable to adequately protect her in the face of the social, economic, and practical realities of renting that she experienced. The following quotations will illustrate.

They had leased my flat for six months. Three days before the fourth month was up, the man said to me casually, "We leave here on the first."

"Your lease?" I replied.

"Lease!" He laughed in my face. "Leases are not worth their ink. Prevent a landlady from turning you out, that's all."

I consulted the lawyer who admitted that leases were all in favour of the tenant. (p. 15.)

And with a different set of tenants:

"The people upstairs have left because of your baby's crying at night. They gave no notice...Another tenant is going too..."

I saw that my notice was being ignored. I had sent it in when I served her last rent. Go she must!...

"You don't mean this?"...

"That notice stands" I said..."I got no notices from the tenants Puss [the crying baby] drove away." (pp. 49-50.)

And with a third group:

"Any caterwauling at nights?"

"We do not keep cats."

"Then you have mice—bound to."

"Please go, I don't want you for tenants."

"Hoity, toity! Give my folks time to look around. They's particular. I telled you so"...

"Ants? Cockroaches?"…

"Go! I won't have you as tenants!"…

Pa roared. "You can't do that! You can't do that! The card says 'Vacant.' We've took it." (p. 69.)

One Way Street

From Carr's perspective, then, the law was one-sided, not so much for the way it was written, but for its one-way enforceability. It could be used against her as "landlord." But it was far more difficult to have it successfully applied against a tenant. So much for her legal power. With regard to her spatial/territorial power, we have already seen that she felt more like a prisoner and serf than a sovereign over her land and tenants. As she elegantly put it:

> Roof, walls, floor can pinch to hurting while they are homing you, or they can hug and enfold. Hurt enclosed is hurting doubled; to spread misery thins it. That is why pain is easier to endure out in the open. Space draws it from you. Enclosure squeezes it close.
>
> …Fate had nailed me down hard. I appeared for the present to have no hammer-claw strong enough to pry myself loose. No, I was not nailed, I was SCREWED into the House of All Sorts, twist by twist…
>
> If only I could have landladied out in space it would not have seemed so hard. The weight of the house crushed me. (p. 13.)

She contrasts this spatial/territorial imprisonment to the tenant's spatial/territorial freedom, or what we refer to elsewhere in the analysis as physical mobility: "The tenant always had this advantage—he could pick up and go. I could not." (p. 13.)

Coercion

Violence and coercive power are not dwelt on at length in our study, although they lurk beneath the surface. At the non-institutionalized level, they can be related to an abuse of personal power in the sphere of landlord-tenant relations, as in other spheres of social face-to-face relations. Carr's history mentions only a couple of instances, both relatively minor. In the first, she had, on the sheriff's instructions, locked out tenants because of unpaid rent and in an attempt to make them pay before re-admittance. (This is a criminal offence now, and subject to stiff penalties.) On the tenant's returning home, the following scene then took place:

> [Tenants] "Open that door! You hear—open that door!"
>
> "When the rent is paid…I am acting under police orders."
>
> "I'll teach you," she said, livid with fury…she had seen her husband coming.

He was a huge man and had a cruel face...He looked a fiend glowering at me and clenching his fists.

"You ___(he called me a vile name)! Open or I will break the door in!" He braced his shoulder against it and raised his great fists. I was just another woman to be bullied, got the better of, frightened.

I ran to the phone. The police came... (p. 35.)

In that case, she was physically intimidated but not assaulted. She would not always be as fortunate:

Bitter cold came. I stuffed the furnace to its limit, hung rugs over north windows...I ploughed through snow which fell faster than I could sweep...My tenants were not entirely dependent on the whims of the furnace, each suite had also an open fire and could be cosy in any weather. Nothing froze except one tap in a north bathroom, the bath of the brutal man—one hand-basin tap. He had hot and cold in his kitchen and bath, but he raved, "this house is unfit to live in. Get a plumber *immediately*."

I said, "That is not possible. People everywhere are without drinking-water, plumbers are racing round as fast as they can. We must manage without one hand-basin for a day or two."

The man followed me into my basement. I did not hear his footfalls in the snow. As I stopped to shovel coal his heavy fist struck across my cheek. I fell among the coal. I stumbled from basement to garden.

"House! House! How long?"...

After twenty-two years I sold the House of All Sorts. (p. 111 and p. 90.)

Why Study Carr's Experience?

We have dealt with Emily Carr's experience at such length for a number of reasons:

- She was a landlady at a time when landladies and landlords were assumed to reign supreme in an unfettered free market and were therefore assumed able to demand extortionate rents and conduct themselves as unscrupulously as the laws then permitted. However, from her account, the free market for the twenty-two-year period from 1913 to 1935 during which she operated appeared to favour the tenant rather than the landlord, in Victoria, B.C., at least, and the old pre-1970s landlord-tenant laws appeared not to have overly favoured the landlord, at least in their implementation, if we are to accept her account as not completely subjective and not unreasonably atypical.

- Carr's pen was able to convey a clear expression of her experience. Very few other small landlords would have had such an ability, if only because the vast majority of them, in Toronto at least, have been first generation immigrants without the use of English as their first language. For example, at the second public meeting of a new association, the Small Landlords Action Committee, a hundred or so small landlords packed a hall to hear the organizers outline their proposed programme. Although the organizer and one or two of his associates spoke English well, the vast majority in the hall found great difficulty in following the discussion, and most stayed among their own ethnic groups, conversing among themselves in their own tongues. It proved impossible to work out a programme at all, because so many of the participants were so full of bitterness, frustration, and hatred that no rational discussion could be maintained. This, together with the language difficulties, made one realize how difficult it would be for small landlords to represent themselves in an effective manner or to find effective spokespersons (let alone to organize effectively). The Babel effect may have had much to do with subsequent low attendance levels.

- Carr had no aspirations to represent ethnic minorities in their landlording operations, but her documenting of her own experiences does provide an invaluable first-hand account of such operations by one who could at least write effectively in her own native language.

- Emily Carr may not have considered herself so, but in a significant sense she was more fortunate than most other small landlords plying their trade. She belonged to the majority ethnic community where she lived, and in addition to having a facility with the common language, she "knew the ropes," so to speak. Being part of the majority culture, she was able with comparative ease to call upon the services of the local policeman and sheriff, and there is evidence throughout her book of a good deal of sympathy among local trades folk (though not the self-acclaimed genteel class including her own family), for their plight. For example, the postman:
      "New to this rentin' bizness, eh? You'll learn-tough yerself to it." His look was kind. (pp. 98-99.)
And, perhaps more importantly, the policeman:
      I ran to the phone. The police came...
      "What do you want me to do?" said the officer.
      "Get them out. I won't house such people. They got away with it in their last place, not here"...

"The town is full of such," said the officer. "House owners are having a bad time. Scum of the earth squeezing into the shoes of honest men gone overseas. How much do they owe?"

I told him.

He went to the man...

"Pay what you owe and get out." (p. 35.)

According to Jamieson's 1967 comprehensive report on Canadian industrial relations, the general conduct of B.C.'s labour organizations, politicians, and even ordinary citizens toward ethnic minorities at that time and even for a little after indicates that if Emily Carr had been an Asian woman plying the same trade in the same place (or in neighbouring Vancouver or any other town in B.C.), we might have expected less sympathy and support from the local community and the forces of law and order. Similarly, had she not been part of the majority community, we can only conjecture how much more insolent, arrogant, and careless of her property her tenants might have been.

In short, tough though some of Carr's experiences doubtless were, we can surmise that among the total multi-ethnic population of small landlords and landladies, she got away pretty lightly. A different, and far more pitiable picture can be seen by any casual observer of the Landlord Self-Help Centre in Parkdale, Toronto. There, again, very few of the "clients" are white English-speaking persons born in Canada. On the three occasions that this author visited the centre prior to spending time there collecting data (to be introduced later in this chapter), the majority of the clients lined up (there has always been a one to three-hour line-up—only one such place to help small landlords exists in Toronto compared to many corresponding centres for tenant aid) were elderly women, speaking in a central or southern European language. In fact, all three people working there are at least bilingual and all belong to ethnic minorities. Many clients come to the centre to discover how to get rid of tenants who are not paying rent and refusing to leave. Although the legal forms and recourses are provided and explained to the clients, a large number of them express fear of the consequences and are dismayed that tenants who have already broken up their apartments and threatened their landlords and landladies with physical violence can legally stay in the building to intimidate the landlady for several more weeks with the protection of the law.

De facto, if not de jure, these women are often helpless. Canny tenants, many of whom, it appears from listening to some of these clients, are young, Canadian born, white, and English-speaking, have access to tenant-help legal clinics with much superior resources, which can help tenants run rings around landladies legally and at no cost to the tenants.

Dependency

As we have seen from these extracts of Emily Carr's *The House of All Sorts*, the usual assumptions of landlord-tenant relations must be reversed. Rather than feeling that her property gave her rights of possession and territory, Carr paints a vivid picture of having her spatial/territorial power taken over by her tenants. She recounts in many scenes the loss of nearly all her privacy on becoming a landlady. Thus her "backstage," with all the significance that Goffman invests in that term, is invaded to the point of virtual loss.

The spatial/territorial power of the tenants over the landlord is linked by Carr irrevocably to their economic power over her or, in the obverse terms stressed by Emerson (1970), by her economic dependence as landlady on her tenants. As she put it "one was dependent on tenants to pay mortgages and taxes" (p. 104). Thus the superiority of economic power, often assumed to be the property of landlords over tenants, is negated by Carr's history.

The low social status of the small landlord is associated with his low sense of social/cultural power and reflected again by his low sense of personal/socio-
-psychological power. All of these are shown by Carr's autobiographical experiences to combine to create a true sense of alienation, according to Marx's (1964) own rich meaning of the term, covering alienation from work (landlord-ing), from associates (tenants), from family (Carr's sisters), and ultimately from self. Carr in fact did suffer from a low sense of self-worth, which her social status as small landlord for some years may or may not have created in the first instance, but certainly aggravated.

Violence

Coercive power is referred to by Carr a couple of times. On one occasion a tenant tried to exercise it against her as landlord, but she was able to enlist the support of the legal custodian of public force, the local constable. On another occasion she was physically assaulted by a tenant, before any public interven-tion could occur. As a woman Carr was more vulnerable to violence from male tenants than a male landlord might have been. But as such she may have enlisted the help of the police more readily. She also trained and kept a large number of very loyal dogs. In short, coercive power at that time did not seem an excessive problem for her.

In fact, for several reasons, she could be considered as presenting a more rosy picture than other landlords would have. She was white and middle-class in a society where being white and middle-class was socially more acceptable than being coloured or working class. She was thus afforded more protection by social convention which was reflected in the attitude of the forces of law and order as well as by tradespeople. She was also able to stand up for herself and to articulate her problems more easily than would a landlord belonging to a recent immigrant community, there being no language or cultural disadvantages. Finally, at that time the law favoured landlords far more than it does now, either in British Columbia or in Ontario. For all these reasons, Carr's account acts as a useful benchmark to measure the power of the landlord in a relatively unfettered situation in the 1930s against his considerably more encumbered position a half-century later.

Small Landlording in Toronto in the Mid to Late 1970s

Introduction: Profile and Limitations of Small Sample

Emily Carr's account of landladying is picturesque and sometimes pathetic in the original sense of the term, but it still paints a rosier picture than would most landladies if they could accurately describe their situation. It is also somewhat out of date. Conditions for small landlords have become considerably tougher since Carr's pre-war landlady days as a result of an intermeshed social, political, legal, judicial, and economic series of processes that will be addressed below. As such, her descriptions may now stand as a precious understatement of current reality.

With Carr's benchmark in mind, an analysis of present-day small landlording is now introduced with the help of the responses to an open-question series of interviews held by the author with ten small landlords who owned properties in or close to the core of downtown Toronto.

A profile of these small landlords is provided in table 1. As can be seen, there were three females and seven males, most of the respondents were 30 to 40 years old, half were single or divorced, and seven of the ten were without dependants. Only two of the respondents were born in Canada, the majority having come from England, Scotland, and Wales.

The responses that produced the data to compile table 1 were the result of fairly obvious questions, where the answer was not already provided by prior knowledge or observation. In almost all cases, respondents were asked how they got into owning rental property (i.e., their motivation for becoming landlords), why they stayed with it, if that was their long-term intention, and what their experiences had been like in running their rental properties. The respondents were told that the results of the interviews would be used for a qualitative research study on small landlords in Toronto. The atmosphere of conducting the interviews was highly informal, and usually involved spending an evening with each landlord in his or her home. In some cases the interviews were conducted at the respondent's place of work, during lunch.

The sample makes no pretense of being representative of small landlords in Toronto. Its size is far too small, and the respondents were not chosen at random from the small landlord population, but were obtained as a result of social networking—hence the preponderance of U.K. immigrants in computer systems and financial occupations among the respondents (the author had these backgrounds at an earlier time). More random representation would have included a far larger proportion of non-United Kingdom ethnic immigrants, a wider age range with a much greater preponderance of older respondents from 50 to 70 years old, a mostly married population with dependents, if they had not yet left home, and a different occupational profile. (See the analysis of the Landlord Self-Help Centre, following.) The interviews, however, would have been far more difficult to conduct, and therefore might have provided less free-flowing perceptual information because in many cases English would not have been the respondent's first language.

In some respects, then, the sample is similar in expectations and experience to Emily Carr's. There was an ease of articulation of a landlord's problems and frustrations because of a facility with the English language. There was also, probably due to reasons already discussed, in most cases a minimum of problems encountered solely as a result of racial, ethnic, and social background, at least in eight out of the ten cases. One might also assume that, insofar as most had university degrees and/or professional qualifications, and some of those employed were in high income brackets, most of the group were privileged socially, educationally, occupationally, and economically, compared to the general population of small landlords represented in the Landlord Self-Help Centre (LSHC) study. This present group's problems, frustrations, and perceptions of impotence might thus be seen as understating the reality that other small landlords, being less privileged, might experience.

Because of all the limitations of representativeness addressed above, the respondents' responses will be used for purposes of illustration only, and no statistical analysis will be attempted. A broader sample of small landlords is used for statistical analysis, gleaned from the summarized records of the LSHC and explained below. Meanwhile, as can be seen from the following, many of the interviews were used by the respondents to "blow off steam," i.e., to recount specific problems with individual tenants and individual situations with city inspectors on work orders. Instead of repeating them individually in detail, they have been edited to omit specifics. A synopsis of these, the most time-consuming components of the interviews, follow.

Synopsis of Some Main Points in Interviews

"The worst part's cleaning up behind them [the tenants]: not just replacing the broken windows, repairing broken doors, filling in chunks of the walls pockmarked by their dart-playing; not even throwing out the furniture of furnished units which they've left in pieces, rugs beered and urinated over till unusable and shameful to keep; no, the worst is less tangible, more personal—the filth that one is forced to face and get rid of; the hundreds of cigarette ends, the stench of smoke and booze, vomit and excrement (usually animal, not human), odours that cling to the walls, the fabrics, and inhabit the rooms for weeks like ghosts

Table 1

Profile of Small Landlords Interviewed in Toronto, Late 1970s

Employed other	Outside Occupation	Sex	Identity	1st Language	Age	Child	Country of Origin	Marital Status	No. of Units	Type of Accommodation
S/E P/T	Computer Programmer/ Systems Analyst	Female	Mo	English	30-40	1	U.S.	Divorced	2	Rooming houses run as "co-ops"; 8-10 tenants
F/T ex	Vice President Finance Multinational Insurance Co.	Male	Vic	English	30-40	—	England	Divorced	3	Rooming houses; 18 tenants
S/E F/T	Carpenter/ Handyperson	Female	Gaye	English	30-40	—	Canada	Divorced	2	Flats in owner-occupied home
—	—	Male	OMH	Polish	70+	—	Poland	Married	12	Flats in converted houses
House-wife	—	Female	Jen	English	20-30	1	Wales	Married	7	Flats in converted houses, one owner-occupied home

F/T	Systems Analyst	M	Andy	English	30-40	—	England	Single	1	Rooming house run as "co-op" 5-6 tenants
F/T	Computer Systems Maintenance	M	Doug	English	30-40	1	Scotland	Married	1	Single-family house rented to group of 3
F/T	Accountant	M	Karl	English	30-40	—	Canada	Married	8	Flats in 2 converted houses
—	Music Student	M	Dave	English	30-40	—	Scotland	Single	12	Apt. building owner-occupied & managed
S/E F/T	Mechanic	M	Abe	Hebrew	30-40	—	Israel	Married	2	Duplex

Source: Primary data collected by author.

from the past; the shamelessness of tenant after tenant, entering a place clean, scrubbed, and often painted, metamorphosizing it into an extension of themselves—so often transient, hence unobliged and unobliging, unloving and unloved; and as a consequence of all this, the feeling of having been let down over and over again—to have trusted and to have had one's trust betrayed.

"The next worst part of a landlord's job must be his constant need to be 'on the job.' A tenant locks herself out at midnight—the landlord is the one to call. Another (or the same one) leaves a tap on in the bath, leaves the stopper in, the bath overflows and, hey presto, a flood: water seeping through three floors and ceilings: fires, fuses, furnace breakdowns, complaints of too much noise from tenants or neighbours; and last, but by no means least, the City, poking in their multiplied unipurpose noses at the least excuse, the slightest provocation, (possibly a tip from a disgruntled tenant, an irritated neighbour): plumbing department, fire department, hydro, health, you name 'em, we got 'em, all nice clean-cut, clean-shaven guys in nice new cars and neat, well-pressed suits, just doing their nicely paid, specialized semi-technical jobs inspecting this sink, following up on that complaint, inspecting hairline cracks in the plaster here, an unpainted drain pipe there, 'regret any inconvenience caused, but have it put right within 30 days, yes what a mess tenants make, we'll be checking back next month. Not done eh? Well, here's the government summons, personally delivered.'[2]

"What we need is time, give us time. Time to get things fixed, time to rent places out, to place ads, to inspect they're in correctly, to take them out when the flat is rented, time to pay bills on time, and, hardest of all, time to arrange appointments with prospective tenants to view. The ratio is around 1:3 of people actually honouring appointments, so to arrange to show a unit to one party provides a 67 percent probability of completely wasting one to three hours, depending on location, plus travelling costs and the loss of telephone calls from other prospective tenants. Hence one tries to cluster as many as possible around a certain hour, but the success of that strategy depends on the level of demand, plus the availability of one's own hours in relation to the enquirers' schedules. In all, the necessity to be in at least two places at the same time, constitutes not just a logistics impossibility but a constant drain on one's energy, a continuous exercise in frustration.

"Anecdote—of one landlady in a decaying Forest Hill mansion, which she had split into six or eight units in addition to the owners' ground floor apartment, who had just succeeded in selling her property, to her intense relief. 'It killed my husband,' she said. He died of a heart-attack in his forties, a senior civil servant who got bogged down in the problems of running a huge, mainly tenant-occupied house, and couldn't cope. He was renovating the ground floor at the time of his thrombosis.

"Collecting rents, dealing with late rent, non-payment, NSF cheques and the like, and eventually giving up on the expectation of ever receiving the rent due, kissing back-rent good-bye, and when the tenants refuse to leave of their own accord, or worse, when they promise to leave but repeatedly break their promise, finally giving up on friendly relations and instituting eviction proceedings; now all according to the law, since circumscription or evasion is a criminal offence, and the first conviction for, say, evicting without court authorization will result normally in a fine, say $2,000, but the second and subsequent convictions may land us as landlord and tenant at the same time, in Her Majesty's non-paying penal institutions. Of course, if the occupant has never had a right to be in his unit, never paid rent, never signed or even verbally arranged a lease, then we landlords can, at our own risk, take advantage of the doctrine of self-help, which means physically evicting the squatter. (We've tried calling on the services and protection of the police, since we read they were there to serve and protect, but they refuse to get involved.) But beware! don't damage a hair on the tenant's precious body, lest you be accused of physical assault. At the same time, try not to get beaten up too badly—a broken nose is tolerable; but brain damage from contacts with heavy objects is hard to repair, and difficult to live with for musical and cerebral types [also for the automobile mechanic to whom, among others, much of the above happened], so perhaps it's best to go easy, accept financial losses, get resigned to those anonymous phone calls that recur throughout the night, threatening you with assault or worse; take out pent-up anger on friends (not many left) and any acquaintances that might care to listen; and leave the prickly stuff to the odd lawyer who might take it, for a moderate fee (most lawyers refuse such messy cases) through the courts again if you've still got energy left, but in any case, hundreds of precious hours wasted, so much of your faith in your fellow man eroded, perhaps beyond the point of redemption, quite aside from the countless numbers of hard-earned dollars lost."

Motivation of the Small Landlord

The foregoing synopsis of interviews represents a thumbnail sketch of some of the roles that these small landlords have played, and some of their subjective feelings—mostly of frustration and alienation from many parts of their community. They are corroborated by other research detailed in appendices B and E. Of course, not all tenants give landlords problems, and in fact some landlords in the interviews mentioned the excellent relations and lasting friendships that had ensued from tenancies. Exact percentages were not offered, but it appeared that 10 to 20 percent of tenancies provided some problems, ranging from recurrently late or NSF rent, to property damage; while a much smaller percentage, probably less than 2 percent, resulted in problems so ugly and intractable that the landlord took legal action.

One of the questions put to all the respondents was what motivated them to become part-time landlords. Although most of the landlords questioned replied on cue "money," often with an embarrassed laugh as though the confession branded them, this does not delve deeply enough into their motivations, and in some cases appears to be because their societal image has been accepted by themselves. To press this issue further, each of the part-time landlords interviewed was asked how much money he or she had gained in the past three years of operations, and each replied that he or she had lost substantial sums, some running to several thousand dollars and cutting significantly into (already taxed) salaried income.

The expectation in most cases, of course, was a realization of substantial capital gains on sale or a large growth in equity, which amounts to the same thing. This expectation, however, often did not take into consideration any new tax measures to hit such "windfall" capital gains (land speculation tax at the provincial level—dramatically imposed in 1975, and capital gains tax at the federal, the combination of which originally aggregated to more than 100 percent of the actual gain in some cases, due presumably to bad mathematical skills and undue zeal on the part of the Ontario provincial government, rather than intended Robin Hood style state communism). In an astonishing number of cases, given the financial background of some of the respondents, neither did calculations of expected capital gains take into account the discounting effects of inflation on real, as opposed to nominal, gains, to borrow from the economists' jargon. And, of course, there is an important economic or analytical reason why landlords who hold onto their properties in the hope of capital gains will be disappointed in this expectation. If rents are constrained, the value of property is thereby also constrained.

An up-to-date statistical analysis of average capital gains from residential rental buildings since the advent of rent controls is provided by Laverty (1982). Suffice to state here that the average gain has been a negative figure.

Opportunity Cost

For most of the part-time landlords interviewed, the expectation of eventual capital gain, whether or not ever realized, did not take into account the opportunity cost of the time and energy spent by landlords in renting, maintaining, and servicing their properties. Obviously, that opportunity cost would have varied greatly. A landlord who was retired and had little else to occupy himself with would have had a different opportunity cost than a young, self-employed professional, who might otherwise have charged clients $50 or more per hour for his time and might have gotten involved in other entrepreneurial dealings reaping more lucrative gains. For other landlords, activities of a more soul-satisfying nature (as in Emily Carr's painting) were sacrificed or severely restricted by landlording responsibilities. So in taking into account not just the purely economic but also more personal considerations, one finds that these part-time landlords perforce sacrificed much of their leisure time and peace of mind and hence their creativity as a direct consequence of their emotionally draining property activities. Thus, while most of the part-time landlords questioned responded that they were in the business for the money, this initial response appeared to just scratch the surface.

Other motivations and explanations, then: several landlords interviewed, though a minority, chose to opt out of a normal work environment with its organizational restrictions, bought one or two houses in order to increase their equity, and planned to subsist on rental income by reducing their costs relative to their revenues. One (not included in table 1) worked three days a week as a musician and was still renovating a second house partially destroyed by tenants the previous year. Another bought two large houses in Parkdale, renovated them herself and was thus able to raise rents considerably, and has now given up full-time professional employment as a computer systems analyst, working part-time only when necessary. (Since completion of the survey, this individual found she had to increasingly subsidize the two houses by part-time computer work. She became disenchanted with such a situation, sold both houses for capital gains sufficient to offset operating loses, though not much more, and moved out of the city to subsistence existence in a mobile home back in her own country. Her re-migration, she explained in 1981 when it occurred, was the result of an increasing sense of alienation and isolation, echoes of Marx once again and Berger too [1967]). A third, a far older man, owned three or four large homes in the Annex, just north of the downtown Toronto core, in which he pottered around and sometimes started fixing up things as the spirit and the authorities moved him. For him, it was already a way of life, part hobby, part business, definitely filling a need to keep occupied and preserve a base of self-worth in his old age.

Short-Term House Speculation and Its Effects

It is worth putting into a historical context the "snap-shot" scenario of landlord attitudes and behaviours outlined in the section above. To many of the part-time landlords interviewed, the purchase of rental property was an attempt to find a channel for economic surplus or disposable wealth which they had accumulated from relatively well-salaried employment incomes. This is not a complete explanation, however, since a far larger segment of the population has disposable wealth than the number who choose to purchase residential rental property. As has already been seen, the purely investment criteria are suspect, but that is only true of the rental and property markets since 1974-75, when the Land Speculation Tax of Ontario (now defunct) and the updated Landlord and Tenant Acts respectively froze the property market (especially for income housing) and arguably changed the power balance between landlords and tenants markedly in the tenants' favour. In the year prior to April 1974, much of the urban population was made aware of the rising price of housing, and many people tried to "cash in" by using disposable income to buy housing, even if rentals would not cover costs, sometimes (though by no means in all cases) in the expectation of a "quick killing" on sale. In summary then, during the heyday of relatively free enterprise in the property market, either short-term or more benignly conceived longer term attempts to acquire a hedge against inflation may have accounted for the greatest number of people purchasing small-scale residential rental income property.

Between 1974 and 1975 (and again, in the latter part of 1981 and throughout 1982), many of those same speculators were caught in a double bind. The selling price of property bought at or near the peak was for some time substantially lower than the purchase price, since the bottom had fallen out of the market. So those speculators who could afford to do so often opted to hold on and sit out the slump. During this period they could no longer accommodate a big gap between property maintenance costs and rental revenue from a finite disposable income borne of limited salaries and other income, so large rent increases became more and more common. This evoked tenant hostility, both in 1974-75 and, to the extent that it was permitted to recur in the face of contemporary rent review legislation, again in 1981-82, which was well publicized by the media and picked up as a potentially useful political issue—hence the Landlord and Tenant Act and rent controls in 1975, the clamouring for a "rent freeze" of 5 percent increases across the land in 1982-83, and, arguably, all the apartment disposal and flip-over events which culminated in the "Cadillac-Fairview debacle" and the two ensuing Royal Commissions of Enquiry, one into the administration of rent review (the long-standing Thom Commission), the other into the financial workings of and institutional controls over trust companies in Ontario.

What have been the effects of this series of developments on landlord-tenant relations? In many cases, landlords were frustrated and bitter that their investments had turned sour. Attention to repairs, regular maintenance, response to tenants' complaints, and general improvements sank to a low ebb. This may have been the consequence of inadequate funds, but might also be attributed to a change of landlord attitude, of greater indifference towards his or her property since it had become less "his" or "hers." There is a growing feeling among landlords that Marcuse and Achtenberg's recommendation that private rental housing be turned into a public utility is gradually becoming the de facto situation, but with none of the security of guaranteed revenues and comfortable employment benefits afforded by government to officers of other "official" public utilities, such as Hydro, Consumer's Gas, and Bell Telephone.

Vandalism

In turn, tenants may have responded by increasing vandalism and vocalization of protest. Very similar dynamics are reported in Sternlieb's study of "The

Tenement Landlord" (1966). In the small pilot study conducted in Toronto in 1983, of the 19 Ontario landlords who responded to a questionnaire (see next section for details), nine reported more major damage and vandalism since 1976, five reported a similar amount, and none reported less. The landlords owned in aggregate 2,298 apartments.

Some indication that landlord-tenant relations have deteriorated since the advent of rent controls is given by responses in the same study. Respondents who were in operation eight years or longer (i.e., since the inception of rent controls in Ontario), were asked whether relations with tenants had improved, stayed the same, or got worse. Eleven (68.8 percent) of the respondents answered that relations had got worse, four (25 percent) stated they had stayed the same, and a solitary one (6 percent) stated they had improved.

Rent strikes have become a common point of discussion (not just on an informal, individual level but as the political strategy of organized tenant groups—see *Shelterforce*, June 1981) and doing a midnight flit when rent is overdue has always been a course of last resort. The climate of landlord-tenant relations can thus, to some degree, be explained as a response to the contemporary developments of the property market. Some of the backwash from this may well have been picked up in the responses to questions summarized earlier from the ten landlords interviewed.

A valid question with regard to the above informal study is how far it can be substantiated by other sources, separated in time and place, but still dealing with the attitudes and perceptions of private residential landlords in the face of a recent imposition of rent controls. A wider questionnaire survey was conducted in Auckland, New Zealand (Lehrer 1984), and is referred to elsewhere in this chapter. The resulting study provided open-ended answers to "Other Comments" solicited from landlord respondents. Of the 138 respondents, 25 provided such comments. They are presented in appendix E in unexpurgated form apart from correction of some grammatical errors. It will be noticed that the tone and tenor of most of the comments tend to corroborate the findings from the more informal Toronto set of interviews conducted several years before and discussed above.

How to Define a Small Landlord

It is evident that the two sources of data used to this point in the chapter refer to what we have termed small landlords. Carr's history deals with a full-time landlady, and the Toronto mini-survey interviewed mostly part-time small landlords. A further, more elaborate private-sector residential landlord classification might take into account the following 12 factors, split into a 4 x 3 matrix, as follows in figure 9.

Figure 9:
Private Sector Residential Landlords Classified by Size,
Time Spent Landlording, and Place of Residence

	No. of Units Managed	Live-in Landlords	Absentee Landlords
1. Full-Time Landlords			
2. Part-Time Landlords			
3. Private Corporate Landlords			
4. Public Corporate Landlords			

The number of units managed will naturally determine whether a landlord is deemed "small" or "large." Lawyer Julius Melnitzer, in a report to the MDSA, (Multiple Dwelling Standards Association[3]) mentioned that the tenants' representatives at the Thom Commission enquiry (where Melnitzer represented the landlords) had suggested that a landlord operating six or more units should be deemed a "large" landlord. This would include landlords such as Emily Carr, and the operators of two triplexes or a rooming house. None of these are reasonably considered large-scale operators. One guiding principle to help designate a small from large operation might be the ability of one normally qualified person, single-handedly, to administer the operation on a full-time basis. Above that level, one cannot consider the operation small. Such a cut-off point might be 30 units, in the case of a residential rental operation, assuming most of the units are concentrated in one physical location. The more scattered, the lower the number of units one person could operate effectively, so there is no one magic number. Similarly, "large scale" does not magically start at 31. It might be reasonable for administrative and other analyses, to posit an intermediate scale of operations where some assistance in physical maintenance and administration is required but full-time professional help has not been hired (12-100 units, depending on concentration of units and abilities of staff and owner). Large-scale might then start from 31 units up (e.g., with a high percentage of high maintenance single-unit dwellings), but usually it would be expected to start above 100 units in larger buildings (see figure 10). The overlap is statistically untidy, but makes more sense of residential rental operations.

Figure 10:
Scale to Designate Small, Intermediate, and Large Scale Private Residential
Landlords

Small		Intermediate		Large
0	12		100	

Description and Analysis of a Small Scale Questionnaire Survey of Private Residential Landlords in Ontario

As part of a multi-faceted research approach to this study, two questionnaires were distributed to a group of private residential landlords who were members of an on-going landlord association. Although it did not represent the largest landlords in the province, the association did include a substantial number of landlords owning in excess of 100 units. It might therefore be considered to reflect not the small landlord discussed to this point and in the LSHC study following, nor the Cadillac-Fairview type of giant landlord played up in the media as an archetypal landlord, but an intermediate between them.

Two questionnaires were distributed to respondents: a long, detailed questionnaire and a shorter summary questionnaire. Since few responses were received in all, and more responses were received from the summary questionnaire, it is this set of responses that is analysed here.

The questionnaire and covering letter are in appendix A. Some 90 questionnaires on landlord activities, socio-economic status (SES), and perceptions were distributed to Ontario residential landlords who were members of the MDSA at their annual general meeting in 1983. According to its president, the MDSA represents landlords owning in total some 30,000 units in Ontario. Fifteen questionnaires were returned completed. An additional ten questionnaires were given to two real estate offices, one in Riverdale, Toronto, the other in Richmond Hill, just north of Toronto. Both offices were branches of large, well established real estate companies. Four further responses were received from this distribution, providing a total of 19 completed questionnaires returned. No attempt was made to keep the four non-MDSA returns separate from the rest. Analysis and summarizing of the responses yielded the following data:

- The mean period that the landlords had owned residential rental property in Ontario was 13.3 years. (Not many short-term speculators among this group. Most of them were in the business before the advent of the 1975 rent controls.)

- The average holding of this group of landlords was 121 rental units. However, this reflects the fact that one respondent owned 1400, another 550, and a third 100 units. The median number of units owned was therefore calculated. It was 12 units. If one omitted from the sample the three "large" landlords mentioned above, the median would drop to 7.5 units, (i.e., sample included a large proportion of small to intermediate landlords, according to the previously defined scale, figure 10).

- Nine respondents lived in their own rental buildings; the remaining ten did not. Although the two largest landlords were "absentee," the landlord owning 100 units did live in his own building.

- The average age of respondents was 49 (almost identical to Sternlieb's finding for Newark [1966] and Lehrer's finding for Auckland [1984B]). Landlording does not appear to be a young person's occupation.

- Eleven of the respondents were married; five were single; three were divorced.

- Respondents in operation eight years or more were asked whether relations with tenants since 1976 had got better, stayed the same, or got worse. Eleven (68.8 percent) responded they had got worse, four (25 percent) responded they had remained the same, and one (6 percent) responded they had got better.

- Respondents were asked if they had experienced more, less, or a similar amount of minor damage by tenants since 1976. Eight (50 percent) responded "similar" and 8 (50 percent) responded "more." None responded "less."

- Respondents were asked if they had experienced more, less, or a similar amount of major damage and vandalism by tenants since 1976. Nine respondents (64.3 percent) reported "more," five (35.7 percent) reported "similar," and none reported "less."

- Respondents were asked to what extent they were able to control expenditures on maintenance and repairs (i.e., apart from essential and emergency expenditures), and whether they planned to increase, decrease, or maintain expenditures at the same level in the long-term. Twelve respondents (66.7 percent) planned to keep them the same and six (33.3 percent) planned to decrease them. None planned an increase. (This is similar to research findings by others, cited in "Power, Participation and the Regulation of Rent," Lehrer, 1984.)

- Thirteen respondents (72.2 percent) reported that the first language of their childhood was English. Three (16.7 percent) reported it was German, one (5.6 percent) that it was Danish, and one (5.6 percent) that it was Polish.

- Eight respondents (47.1 percent) reported that their mother's first language was English; four (23.5 percent) that it was German; two (11.8 percent) that it was Polish; one (5.9 percent) that it was "Jewish" (presumably meaning Yiddish); one (5.9 percent) that it was Danish; and one (5.9 percent) that it was French. Thus, in all, over half (52.9 percent) the respondents reported a language other than English as the mother's language. (In this small sample the majority of landlords could be considered to belong to ethnic minorities.)

- Eleven of the 19 respondents (57.9 percent) reported having approached their local alderman, MPP, or MP for advice and assistance on problems related to their residential rental property. Of these, none found the officials extremely helpful, none found them helpful, four (36.4 percent) found them unhelpful, and six (54.5 percent) found them extremely unhelpful.

- Rental income/loss was asked for in large income brackets, and many years' responses were missed, so mathematical averaging of income per year has not been attempted. However, the trends of net rental losses compared to positive rental income over the nine years reported is noteworthy:

	No. of respondents reporting positive income	No. of respondents reporting losses	Total
1974	5	2	7
1975	5	2	7
1976	5	2	7
1977	5	2	7
1978	6	2	8
1979	7	4	11
1980	6	5	11
1981	6	7	13
1982	5	7	12

While the number reporting positive net income remained quite constant throughout the nine-year period, the number reporting losses increased from two to seven. The total numbers are of course very small, but as a proportion 71 percent of respondents reported a net rental income in 1974 (the year before rent controls) compared to 29 percent reporting a loss. By 1982 the proportion reporting income had dropped to 42 percent, and those reporting a loss had increased to 58 percent.

Because the total number of respondents was very small, it would not be appropriate to deal at length with the results of the survey. It was intended to illustrate and to provide some limited and tentative substantiation for other material presented in this chapter, but not to form the basis of substantial data analysis. However, further research in the area would certainly be helpful in establishing the validity or otherwise of the findings presented here.

Notes

1. Achtenberg (1973 A, B, C) on the U.S. scene; Marcuse (1979), specifically on New York City; the Community Research and Publications Group (1973) on Massachusetts; Cutting (1974) on Great Britain; Social Planning Council of Metropolitan Toronto (1974) on Toronto; Wheeler (1969) on Montreal; Bureau of Municipal Research (1977) on Toronto; and Patterson & Watson (1976) on Canada in general.

2. As even the Bureau of Municipal Research (1977) noted in its study of the increasing shortage of rental housing in Toronto: "One criticism of by-law enforcement in recent years has been the number of inspections that must be carried out, each by a different inspector." (p. 21.)

   Some understanding of the difficulties encountered by small landlords is implicit in other statements:

   > The City should adopt...a policy to support landlords who lack the financial resources and technical ability to comply with standards enforcement...The City has already developed a policy of offering technical advice to non-profit housing groups; it might wish to consider broadening this policy and extending it to include small landlords who express an interest in learning how to manage residential property. (p. 21.)

   The intention was clearly noble, but still smacked of a "white man's burden" or noblesse oblige. The implication is that the City will know better how to manage residential property. The difference in the financial, legal, administrative, and socio-psychological power bases of the City as compared to the individual small landlord, and how these will affect their relative abilities to manage residential property, is not addressed. Equally ignored are the issues of landlord ethnicity, cultural values, and language difficulties, and how these will affect the extent to which the general population of small landlords would "express an interest in learning how to manage." It could be that the City has more to learn from small ethnic landlords about what is really involved in managing residential property than vice versa.

3. The fact that what is in reality a landlord's association feels the need to call itself something with no reference whatever to being landlords, is itself a strong indication of the shyness felt by landlords of advertising their occupation, possibly for reasons of perceived delegitimation, marginality of political and social status, and the stigmatization described elsewhere in this study.

CHAPTER 4

Ethnic Minorities as Small Landlords

Canada, the United States, the United Kingdom, and New Zealand

One of the few landlord studies with a sociological rather than an economic focus concerning Canadian data is Krohn et al.'s (1979) Montreal study. It shows that in what might be called normal market conditions (i.e., those that are neither highly speculative nor part of a post-speculative slump with exacerbating government controls), specifically identifiable ethnic and social groups tend to become small-time landlords. Krohn et al. split up the groups in Westmount, Quebec, between Canadian, Jewish, and new immigrants. Most of the French and English Canadians of post-second generation had moved out of the area studied and sold their properties. Some first and second generation Jews had stayed and rented part of their homes, others had moved, while retaining the properties and renting them out. New immigrants had tended to replace the WASP English, French Catholic, and Jewish residents, and currently represented a large portion of both owners and tenants.

Both the Milner Holland Committee report (1965) and Rex & Moore's Birmingham housing study (1967) note the same over-representation of ethnic immigrants among the small landlord population in the United Kingdom. The former provided a survey of the London private rental market, showing that 51 percent of this rental sector was owned by individual landlords, the rest by corporations, charities, the Church of England, etc. The individual landlords were further split into absentee landlords ("extra-mural"), owner-occupier, and tenant landlord. The group most closely related to the study of small landlords would be the owner-occupier landlords. Of these, 49 percent were of British origin, 15 percent were from the West Indies, Pakistan, India, or West Africa, 5 percent were from other parts of the Commonwealth, and a large 31 percent were from other countries ("mainly European"). The degree of over-representation is indicated by the fact that at that time the coloured population of Britain was estimated at less than 2 percent of the total population (Burney 1967, p. 3). Burney described the U.K. situation graphically as follows:

For this reason [discrimination], and through their own group network, immigrant landlords have become a major source of accommodation for immigrant tenants. Indeed it is hardly an exaggeration to say that they are the only people who see a point at all in increasing their interest in cheap rental property, and this is particularly true of certain ethnic groups—Sikhs and Maltese for example—among the immigrants. This is not philanthropy: it is a market in which a living can be made, or at least a supplementary income, in a way which the immigrant can easily understand and in which he can become practised without reference to the twilight zone and the people in it. *Yet having once adopted this role, the landlord at once inherits the mantle of stricture and restriction* of exploiting and being exploited, which is the unhappy character of the part. The most telling image thrown up in the study of a twilight area of Birmingham by Professor John Rex and Mr. Robert Moore was the *"scapegoat landlord,"* the man who adopts a despised role, providing for despised people, and on whom society wreaks its vengeance by applying sanctions designed to limit that role. While this is a melodramatic way of describing such mundane activities as the enforced installation of lavatories at the request of the public health department, it has the ring of truth: for the landlord is blamed and punished for doing his job badly whilst denied the incentives to do it well. (Burney 1967, 11-12.)

Scapegoating

The phenomenon of scapegoating has recently been re-discovered in a more general context and labelled "blaming the victim."

In Sternlieb's *The Tenement Landlord* (1966), the two important issues of size of holdings of landlords and their ethnic backgrounds are investigated. With regard to the first, he states:

The much-publicized concept of the "slumlord" relies on the supposition that there are a small number of individuals who own the bulk of the slum tenements. While large owners are far from an insignificant proportion of total ownership, as the research presented have indicated, the degree of concentration is much overstated. This is far from unique to Newark. For example, in Grebler's (1952) study of ownership in New York's Lower East Side, there is a strong indication that small holdings predominate...

Over 40 per cent of the Newark parcels, for which interviews were secured, are in the possession of landlords who own no other rental property. Less than a quarter are owned by landlords possessing over six parcels of this type. (pp. 121-22.)

Sternlieb's findings on small holdings are similar to those in a recent Auckland study (Lehrer 1984). Many of the reasons given for ownership are similar. Sternlieb states:

> Many of the owners interviewed in the course of this study are owners by default rather than by purpose; are owners by inheritance; or by lack of purchasers to buy unwanted properties...(p. 124.)

With regard to the ethnicity of his tenement landlord sample, Sternlieb disappointingly only classifies by three categories "Negro, Puerto Rican, and Other white." The data in any case are as follows:

Table 2
Landlord Ethnicity of Tenement Buildings in Newark

		%
Negro	129	33.4
Puerto Rican	5	1.3
Other white	252	65.3
Total	386	100.0

Source: Exhibit 6-11, in Sternlieb's *The Tenement Landlord* (1966), p. 136.

Although no census data are available for Ontario, studies by Burney (U.K.), Krohn and Tiller (Montreal), Rex and Moore (U.K.), and to a smaller extent Sternlieb (Newark) lend some credence to the visual observation that the more recently arrived immigrants of the mainly ethnic communities in Toronto, especially the Greek, Italian, Portuguese, Chinese, and more recently East Indian communities, may have provided much of the rental accommodation on a shared/split-house basis as small tenement-type landlords, especially in the city core. As Burney puts it as a comment on the U.K. experience:

> This [Milner Holland] survey backs up the impression that letting off part of one's own house is an immigrant characteristic, in which the coloured groups here followed in the footsteps of Poles, Jews and others. (p. 13.)

Immigrant Landlords

Why do some immigrants choose to be landlords? Again for questionably sound economic reasons, but in addition and perhaps more fundamentally, for socio-cultural and socio-psychological reasons grounded ultimately in notions of power. The financial reasons are of course that the rental income is expected to help "carry" the house. The socio-cultural and socio-psychological reasons are to do with the status of being a property-owner. One of the most significant symbols of prestige, status, and security in the communities of origin among the ethnic minorities may have been that of owning one's own property. (See for example Howe's *World of Our Fathers*, 1976.) Therefore, to really feel one had "made it" in the new country, a new immigrant might feel a powerful urge to buy a home, even if he or she could not afford to carry it initially on his or her own income—hence the proportion of part-time residential landlords who belong to ethnic minorities. The sense of spatial/territorial power might not be without its difficulties either, but it might still present more tangible evidence of belonging than most other power bases accessible to ethnic immigrants, and as such have a value that exceeds or overrides the purely economic value of owning a property. The experience of dispossession as refugees from a previous country may heighten the psychological need to regain tangible property in a new host country. This may help explain the large number of European Jews among the landlord populations of the United Kingdom, the United States, New Zealand, and possibly Canada.

The social-psychological factors have to do with rental patterns observable in Toronto, but are corroborated in both the United Kingdom and Montreal studies. Each ethnic minority tends to have a strong preference to rent to members of its own group, thus creating a more certain supply of housing for the latest new immigrants from that community and also reducing the chances of deeply felt mutual hostility, suspicion, and hence generally bad tenant-landlord relations. Territorial security at least as much as territorial power might thus provide a strong motivation for large homeownership with the consequent ability to provide secure rental accommodation, free from discrimination, to one's own ethnic minority group. Rents in these situations might tend also to be somewhat less than market rate, according to Krohn and Tiller, since purely economic criteria are not the only ones being used. As Burney puts it:

> An immigrant house owner may often have motives other than purely financial for taking tenants, especially when these are his own countrymen, perhaps kinsmen, who would otherwise have nowhere to go. There is a marked tendency for people of the same origin to stick together in one house... (pp. 13-14.)

> Ill will flourishes among landlords and tenants of different ethnic groups, as a visit to any furnished rent tribunal in any large city will reveal...Uncomfortable relations always tend to breed when the landlord is landlord within his own home: where people of strange origin are involved, the friction is compounded. (p. 14.)

No Historical Departure

Virtually the same phenomenon was apparent as early as the turn of the century for United Kingdom immigrants to Canada, who are not now normally considered ethnic immigrants since their successors have been able to assimilate relatively easily and successfully into the host society. However, on first coming over, the English were readily distinguishable and not yet "at home." So rental properties run by the English for the English, were quite popular, as Ross McCormack notes (1981):

> English boarding houses...were an extension of chain migration. In the same way that such institutions provided Harney's Italians with "a means of living with one's own," they furnished English immigrants who did not enjoy access to a familial home with emotional, and frequently material support. Boarding houses were of course, primarily commercial enterprises but they prospered by offering English immigrants familiar, often familial, environments...Like families, boarding houses facilitated the immigrants' economic adjustment. A Lancashire man who arrived in Winnipeg when "times were bad" remembers securing work under the auspices of fellow boarders at an English establishment in the city's West End. (p. 45.)

The English immigrants were, however, a fairly privileged class, whatever the economic conditions. Their citizenship, until the 1970s, was automatic and there was never any question of their political and legal rights. They were able to jump into the centre of social and political power with very few barriers to climb, so one does not find many small landlords among them, or operators of marginally profitable and socially-stigmatized rooming or boarding houses, as the social and political climate grew increasingly hostile towards landlording, and as the laws were gradually changed to reflect that hostility. (Many of the U.K. immigrants in the landlords' open-ended interviews have now at time of writing disposed of their rental "investment" properties.)

Upward Mobility?

This filtering-up process, known more familiarly as upward social and economic mobility, may have been the norm for the English immigrants but was not so easy for other immigrants. Instead, one sees the less protected and less powerful ethnic minorities taking over the low-prestige, low-status, low-power roles of shopkeeper, laundry operator, restaurant operator, and landlord, where they could be harassed by many levels of society with relative impunity. Not all provinces were as blatant in their discrimination as B.C., which legally prevented its Chinese community from practising any of the major professions since licensing depended on voting status, and until the 1940s the vast majority of the Chinese community were denied the right to vote. As Edgar Wickberg

(1981) points out, not only were they denied voting rights at the provincial level but also at the federal and municipal levels. Such exclusion from any sphere of political influence and power not surprisingly made them ripe for discrimination and vulnerable to attack by the host community. For example, Wickberg writes: "The Vancouver Anti-Oriental Riot of 1907 destroyed a great deal of property in Chinatown and threatened the lives of the inhabitants." (op. cit., p. 173.)

Discrimination

Lack of municipal representation rendered the Chinese impotent to contest exclusion from even occupations other than the most prestigious, well-paid, and powerful professional jobs. As Wickberg notes:

> There were also innumerable efforts to exclude the Chinese from various occupations. In various parts of Canada, complex municipal ordinances harassed the hand-laundry operator. Provincial and municipal legislation attempted to prevent white women from working as waitresses in Chinese-owned restaurants. By legislation or organized interest group campaigns, efforts were made to remove the Chinese from work in the extractive industries and to curb the growth of Chinese-operated vegetable farming operations. (ibid.)

All the normal power bases available to communities—legal, economic, political, and social, were, then, denied the Chinese community and other ethnic minorities. ("No Jews, Negroes or Dogs" was a public notice on Toronto beaches, still remembered by citizens growing up in the 1940s.) So it is not surprising that, despite the drawbacks and vulnerabilities already illustrated, they would cling to small-scale property ownership and renting as a meagre source of income, security, and territorial power, despite the possibilities of its destruction or confiscation by the host community—e.g., in the case of the Japanese community. As Ann Gomer Sunahara notes (1981):

> Beginning in February 1942, 20,881 Japanese Canadians were uprooted from their homes, stripped of all real and personal property, and confined, at their own expense, in government detention camps. (p. 254.)

This may help explain why the host community has been quick to condemn, has put difficulties in the small landlord's way, and has provided increasingly protective legislation to its predominantly white English-speaking private tenant population. As John Wood comments (1981):

> The time has come to recognize the significant increase in Canadian citizens of Asian, African, Caribbean and Latin American origins and to understand the special problems of adjustment they face here. Many find themselves on the defensive

against racist abuse in public and discriminatory treatment by government officials or agents of the law. In their view, the political system is populated almost entirely by whites, most with scant knowledge about or interest in...the needs of visible minorities. The latter have few effective links to the political system, few spokesmen inside the system who can articulate their needs and extremely little political influence. (p. 178.)

His comments can be extended to the other ethnic minorities who may comprise the majority of small landlords, even though this fact is very rarely publicly discussed, especially in debates on equity between landlord and tenant.

Paternalism

Three separate visits to the courts in Toronto indicated that in cases brought by the city housing inspectors (plumbing, electrical, health, etc.), the overwhelming majority of defendants were ethnic immigrants. While in some cases the magistrate was sympathetic, in most his manner was paternalistic. He was white and spoke English with a confident Canadian accent. Apposite in this context are the following quotes from *Housing on Trial* (Burney 1967):

"Parading immigrant landlords in court" was a practice for which Birmingham City Council was taken to task by the authors of the Sparkbrooke Study [Rex and Moore 1967]. By 1966 as much as 98 percent of all legal action against landlords in Birmingham had been taken against Indian and Pakistani landlords...There are many downright bad coloured landlords; on the other hand, because of their visibility and because they are mostly "small men," living on or near the spot, they are easier to lean on than the man of straw, the well-defended company, or the hard-to-trail absentee owner. (pp. 25-26.)

Individual public health inspectors are frequently on decent personal terms with individual coloured landlords, whom they often find docile and anxious to co-operate...nevertheless there is a noticeable "colonial style" in many inspectors' approach to immigrant landlords and tenants which is markedly different from their manner to English people—who respond to them quite differently. (p. 30.)

An extract of the research on the ethnic status of private residential landlords in Auckland, New Zealand, conducted in early 1984 on behalf of the New Zealand National Housing Commission is given in appendix D. The general survey research found that in the respondent sample of some 140 residential landlords in the Auckland region, the proportion of respondents admitting to non-Maori minority ethnic status was seven times higher than the proportion of non-Maori minority ethnic persons in the general population, according to the latest New Zealand Year Book: appendix E records a series of interviews with some of the leaders in the Indian community apropos the residential landlording activities of the community. It tends to confirm some of Rex's findings (1967, 1970). However, there are some attenuating circumstances discussed in the appendix (especially the very small overall proportion of ethnic minorities in the overall population) which may well explain why the landlording scene in Auckland is more benign and, so far, less stringently controlled by government than has been reported for jurisdictions elsewhere in this study.

The Power of Ethnic Minorities in Ontario

It is suggested here that ethnic and other minorities might have a less than powerful voice in housing policy and specifically in private rental housing law and its administration. This is because they have been under-represented in the public and especially the parliamentary political system, and have therefore had little power over legislation which might adversely affect them. In order to test this hypothesis for Ontario, in 1983 the three political party caucuses were contacted at Queen's Park and asked for a break-down of the current ethnic composition of their membership. Although nothing official was offered, the Liberal caucus office informally advised that eleven of their MPPs had ethnic minority backgrounds, as follows:

Italian	3	German	2
French-Canadian	2	Polish/Ukrainian	1
Polish/German	1	Norwegian	1
Dutch	1		

The NDP caucus advised at that time that the only MPPs who were not white Anglo-Saxons were three MPPs of Italian background. The Conservative caucus, instead of providing unofficial data, was good enough to provide the complete alphabetical list of members of the Ontario legislature, together with the official "Biographical Sketches of Members." Accordingly, this author used the sketches to create an analysis of the membership by age, ethnic origin, and religion, as far as they could be determined by the sketches. Only 96 out of the 125 MPPs were "old" members—those newly elected did not have sketches, and therefore do not form part of our analysis—this helps explain some discrepancy between our results and those provided informally by the two opposition party caucuses.

However, the pattern that emerges is similar to what one might have been led to expect: English-speaking Canadians of Anglo-Saxon stock comprise the great majority of the MPPs, i.e., four out of five, and most of those professing religion preferred some brand of Protestantism, the United Church being the favourite. However, Catholics and Roman Catholics comprised a healthy quarter of the total MPPs in the analysis. No Moslems, Buddhists, or more esoteric religions such as the Bahai faith were represented, and perhaps more surprisingly, only one religiously professing Jew. See table 3 for the ethnic distribution of Ontario MPPs, and table 4 for their age, religion, and ethnic origin.

Table 3
Ethnic Origins of Ontario MPPs, 1983

No.	Ethnic Origin	%
4	French Canadian	4.4
5	Italian	5.5
1 1/2	Polish	1.6
1 1/2	Ukrainian	1.6
3	German	3.3
2	Jewish	2.2
1	U.S.	1.1
1	Dutch	1.1
20	U.K./Irish	22.0
52	English Canadian	57.1
91	Total classified	99.9

Source: Ontario Legislature, "Biographical Sketches of Members," 1983, plus verbal information from three party caucus offices at Queen's Park.

The omissions are perhaps more important than the distribution shown in the table above: there was apparently not one Portuguese, Spanish, or Greek representative in the assembly, which indicates the paucity of representation of recent southern European immigrant communities. Perhaps even more telling was the absolute lack of representation for blacks, Chinese, Japanese, and East Indians.

In September 1990 a new provincial government was elected in Ontario, giving the NDP power for the first time. The MPPs appear far more representative of ethnic minorities than in any previous Ontario legislature. Since they have yet to convene in Parliament, we have still to see how the change in representation will affect rental housing policy.

Protecting the Weak?

Immigrants will acquire social power wherever they can, and if access to some areas is more difficult, if not totally barred, they may initially choose those with easier access, or fewer barriers, such as trade, small business, and property owning and renting. But they manifestly have such negligible political power with which to protect their interests, that it may be easier for elected repre-

Table 4

Ontario MPPs by Age, Religion, and Ethnic Origin

Age	31-40	41-50	51-60	61-70	71+
Born	1943-52	1933-42	1923-32	1913-22	1912 or before
Number	18	25	29	13	2

Religion										
United Church	Catholic	Roman Catholic	Anglican	Baptist	Unitarian	Presbyterian	Protestant	Jewish	Lutheran	No church Given
33	13	13	9	2	1	4	4	1	2	18

Ethnic Group									
English (UK)	French (Continent)	Irish (UK)	Italian	Polish	Ukrainian	German	Jewish	U.S.	Dutch
52	4	20	5	1½	1½	3	2	1	1

Source: Province of Ontario: Parliamentary Guide—"Biographical Sketches of Members," 1983.

sentatives to follow the path of least resistance, and to yield to majority pressure, with a legitimizing social welfare argument. In doing so they will acquiesce in, if not positively favour such legislation as rent controls, and ride roughshod mainly over the interests of the least articulate. Those advocating controls would indeed assert that the legislation protects the least powerful. However, other studies (Lehrer 1984A) have shown that while this might have been the intention, it has not been the effect.

Immigrants learn fast, and it is not surprising that the second and third generations of Jews, Germans, Poles, and Chinese are less interested in those economic activities that attract social stigma and are less protected by the system of government and public administration, such as rental housing, and increasingly interested in gaining high professional status as a means not only of greater security and economic power but of higher social status, and thus ultimately gain access to their fair share of political power. (This may help explain the high average age of landlords, including small landlords in all recent studies.)

We have been discussing the relative security with which an individual from an ethnic minority plies his trade, whether it be landlording or some other trade that has frequent public contact and puts property at risk. It is therefore pertinent to ask to what degree ethnic minorities are represented among those whose work puts them the most at risk: the police force, whose primary role is ostensibly to provide protection for property and person. The Metro Toronto police force was therefore contacted to ascertain the ethnic origin of its members, but the officers stated they were unable to provide such information. Similarly, the Ontario Provincial Police was contacted, but with the same negative results. In fact, one of the persons contacted at the OPP was the secretary to the task force of the Ontario Ministry of the Solicitor-General, which recently published a report recommending higher representation of ethnic minorities in the Ontario police forces. But neither the report nor the secretary were able to provide data on ethnic representation in the forces. One of the Metro police representatives was pleased to advise that 3.3 percent of the force consisted of what he called "visible minority" persons. However, apart from one or two black faces in Metro, this author has yet to see a clear manifestation of diverse ethnic representation among the police forces of Ontario. In a *Globe and Mail* article, "Hill says text on race not enough for police" (17 July 1983), it was reported that "less than 3 percent of Metro Toronto's 5,000 member force is non-white, although between 15-20 percent of the general population is made up of visible minorities." The same article also stated that the OPP did not know how many of its 4,200 officers were non-white.

In a pluralist democracy, those groups with representatives in legislative assemblies are assumed to have some access to political and legislative power. In such a democratic system, the means of coercive power is assumed to reside for most domestic purposes in the police force, which derives its legitimization as an instrument of law and order because it is expected to enforce public administration and policy. Within these positions of political/legislative and public coercive power, there would appear to be a very substantial under-representation of the many ethnic minorities who appear to comprise the majority of the small landlords.

CHAPTER 5

The Landlord Self-Help Centre, Toronto, 1978 to 1983

Introduction

It has been stated previously that the majority of small landlords in Toronto are not white Canadians speaking English as their first language. Visits to the courts which spend so much of their time dealing with landlord-tenant matters will quickly corroborate this casual observation. A more comprehensive source of data, however, is the Landlord Self-Help Centre, located in Parkdale, Toronto, and set up in the mid-1970s by a very socially conscious ethnic immigrant with a heavy accent and a concern that, while tenants who were oppressed by landlords could go to one of many government-supported legal aid clinics, landlords had no such place to turn to when they were cheated or exploited by their tenants. Although in an interview granted before she died, she admitted some landlords were able, financially or otherwise, to fend for themselves, she still asserted strongly that most were not in that fortunate position.

Summary records of all the clients helped in the centre were made available for the purposes of this study, for the periods April 1978 to March 1979, January 1980 to December 1980, May 1981 to April 1982, and May 1982 to April 1983. Thus a period of five years is straddled, with summary data provided for all the clients helped in the 48 months covered.

Trends in Ethnic Composition of Small Landlords

One notes from table 5 that over the five-year period, in aggregate, just one in three small landlord clients spoke English as their mother tongue, one in ten spoke Polish, and almost one in ten spoke Italian. The rest were smaller minorities, but those using languages other than English, or the foreign ones specified, comprised over one in four of the total of 5,625 clients helped during the five-year period.

Table 5

Total Number of Clients of LSHC Categorized by Mother Tongue Spoken, 1978-83

Mother Tongue Spoken	1978-79		1980		1981-82		1982-83		Total	
	No.	%	No.	%	No.	%	No.	%	No.	%
English	319	37.9	423	33.3	612	35.2	584	32.9	1938	34.4
Polish	107	12.7	159	12.5	154	8.8	156	8.8	576	10.2
Ukrainian	42	5.0	79	6.2	94	5.4	86	4.8	301	5.3
Yugoslavian	46	5.5	52	4.1	52	3.0	59	3.3	209	3.7
Chinese	42	5.0	75	5.9	107	6.1	124	7.0	348	6.2
Italian	47	5.6	120	9.5	170	9.8	189	10.0	526	9.3
Portuguese	27	3.2	48	3.8	74	4.3	73	4.1	222	3.9
Other	211	25.1	313	24.7	478	27.5	506	28.5	1508	26.8
Total No. of Clients	841	100.0	1269	99.9	1741	100.1	1777	99.4	5628	99.8

Source: LSHC Summary Records, 1978-83.

Of equal significance, perhaps, is an underlying trend: The English-speaking groups comprised 37.9 percent of the total client population in 1978-79, but this had dropped to 32.9 percent of the total by 1982-83, a relative drop of 15 percent from their original proportion. Analysis of the Census of Canada census tracts reveals by comparison that the mother tongue of 71.26 percent of the population of the Toronto Census Metropolitan Area (CMA) was English. To put it the other way round, according to Canada census figures, 28.74 percent of the Toronto CMA population spoke a language other than English as their mother tongue. According to the LSHC records, 67.1 percent of their clients spoke a language other than English as their mother tongue. This represented a proportion 2.33 times larger than that of the general population.

The proportion of Polish-speaking small landlord clients had also dropped substantially over the period: from 12.7 percent of the total in 1978-79 to only 8.8 percent in 1982-83, a drop of 31 percent from their original proportion. The Yugoslavian- and Ukrainian-speaking clients had also dropped in their proportions: the Yugoslavs by a considerable and the Ukrainians by a less significant proportion, but the total numbers they represent are small.

On the other hand, the Portuguese, the Chinese, the Italian, and those lumped together who spoke other foreign languages have all increased their proportion of the total small landlord client population, in addition to increasing substantially in absolute numbers.

Inferences

What might one infer from this detailed analysis of landlords' ethnicity? To the extent that the clients of the LSHC represent the total population of small landlords, one might have evidence of a trend of earlier immigrant groups, especially the English, Polish, and Yugoslav speaking-groups, turning away from operating as small landlords, and possibly away from the Parkdale/West Toronto area, and being replaced by other, newer groups of immigrants such as the Chinese, Portuguese, Italians, etc. This is consistent with the findings of Krohn and Tiller, and with research done in the U.K. On the other hand, one might also explain the trends not by changes in the total small landlord population, but simply by the fact that newer immigrants, new to the landlording game, are likely to have more landlording problems than English-speaking and experienced landlords. Although this interpretation is plausible too, it does not rule out the validity of the first since they are not mutually exclusive. In the absence of more conclusive data, one might bear both explanations in mind.

Some other qualifications of the data group: The large proportion of clients whose mother tongue is English should not conjure up an image of all descendants being from English, Irish, Scottish, and Welsh stock. Included among this group must be the black community, the Jewish community to the extent that their mother tongue is not Yiddish or some other foreign language, and other ethnic minority groups whose first language happens to be English. Thus the total number might conceal two trends—a strong downward trend in numbers of small landlords of Anglo-Saxon stock, concealed somewhat in our statistics by an upward trend in small landlords of other ethnic minorities whose mother tongue has been given as English.

It should also be noted that second generation immigrants are not picked up by the LSHC data. A significant proportion of the English-speaking small landlord clients may be Chinese, Japanese, East Indian, Italian, and German Canadians; born and schooled in Canada, their first language is therefore English, but their ethnic identity still belongs to the minority groups, both in their own perception and in that of others.

Family Status, Family Size, and Age Profile of Small Landlords

To some extent this hypothesis that new and second generation immigrants make up an increasingly larger proportion of the small landlord population is confirmed by analysis of the family status data, summarized in table 6.

The absolute number of widowed clients peaked at 129 in 1981-82 (7.4 percent) and fell to 100 in 1982-83 (5.8 percent). Clearly it is not possible to argue from the data that the vast majority of small landlords are really little old widows! However, it is evident from the data that an increasing proportion of the small landlords in the sample have a larger-than-average number of dependants. In 1979-80, 136 clients had from three to five dependants. By 1982-83 the number of these clients had jumped to 404. In terms of the proportions to the total number of clients in each year, the rise is still large, from 16.2 percent of the total clients in 1978-79, to 23.2 percent in 1982-83, or 43.2 percent above the 1978-79 proportion. The rise is also evident in each period. Clearly, then, the family size of the small landlord clients has been getting larger, and this suggests a greater preponderance of new immigrants who traditionally have had larger family sizes. For purposes of comparison to the general population, analysis of the 1981 Census of Canada shows that for the Toronto CMA, of the 785,400 families only 15.3 percent had three or more children living at home. Cross (1978) found large family size to be related to ethnicity in his U.K. private residential landlord study, and makes the following relevant comment about family size:

> We have already seen the contribution which large families, large households and a large number of dependants per wage-earner makes to disadvantage in the field of housing. However, it would be a mistake to presume that these are the only significant reasons which contribute to the disadvantage of ethnic minorities in this field. (p. 64.)

One could surmise that the dependants in the LSHC sample belonged to particular marital status groups and therefore exclude others (e.g., the single

Table 6

Marital Status and Number of Dependants of LSHC Clients, 1978-83

Marital Status	1978-89 No.	1978-89 %	1980 No.	1980 %	1981-82 No.	1981-82 %	1982-83 No.	1982-83 %	Total No.	Total %
Single	139	16.5	204	16.1	289	16.6	299	17.2	931	16.7
Married	563	66.9	846	66.7	1132	65.0	1154	66.4	3694	66.1
Divorced	35	4.2	54	4.5	93	5.3	89	5.1	271	4.8
Separated	36	4.4	76	6.0	98	5.6	97	5.6	308	5.5
Widowed	67	8.0	89	7.0	129	7.4	100	5.8	385	6.9
Total	840	100.0	1269	100.3	1741	99.9	1739	100.1	5589	100.0
Number of Dependants										
3 to 5	136	16.2	264	20.8	394	22.6	404	23.2	1198	21.4
6 and more	13	1.5	18	1.4	25	1.4	23	1.3	79	1.4
Total no. of clients with 3+ dependants	149	17.7	282	22.2	419	24.0	427	24.5	1277	22.8

Source: LSHC Summary Records, 1978-83.

Table 7

Age of Clients at LSHC
(1981 Census Data)

AGE	1978-79		1980		1981-82		1982-83		Toronto CMA	
	No.	%	No.	%	No.	%	No.	%	%Total	%15+
50-64	257	30.6	343	27.0	490	28.1	565	31.8	14.89	18.70
65+	87	10.3	217	17.1	253	14.5	239	13.4	9.13	11.47
Total 50+	344	40.9	560	44.1	743	42.6	804	45.2	24.02	30.17

Source: LSHC Summary Records, 1978-83, and 1981 Census of Canada, cat. no. 95-977, vol. 3.

and widowed), and thus by reducing the denominator arrive at a higher proportion of clients with large numbers of dependants. However, there is no certainty that none of the single or widowed clients have dependants. Therefore, the total number of clients has been used as the denominator. This problem of course is caused by having only summary data to work with, which prevents the possibility of extensive sub-classification (e.g., singles with dependants, etc.).

Analysis of the age profile of clients, as shown in table 7, suggests that for the time being the proportion of senior citizens has levelled off and is declining a little, but the combined proportion of 50 to 64 year olds and those over 65 in the total client population has risen from 40.9 percent in 1978-79 to 45.2 percent in 1982-83. In any case, nearly half the small landlords needing help in this summary were either approaching or already beyond retirement age. As shown in table 7, these figures compare with percentages in the general population of the Toronto CMA, per 1981 Census of Canada data: of the 24 percent total of those 50 years old and over, 14.9 percent were in the 50 to 64 age range, and 9.1 percent were in the 65+ group. (Simple proportional interpolation of aggregate census age groups was made, in order to compute a comparable age range). If one excludes from the total Toronto CMA population those aged under 15, as seems reasonable, and is compatible with our analysis of comparative income figures, the age percentages rise to 18.75 percent and 11.5 percent respectively, and 30.25 percent combined. They are still both by individual classification and as a combined percentage substantially below the percentages of older persons acting as small landlords in the LSHC client population.

Aggregate Income and Employment Status of Small Landlords

One final, and possibly the most contentious piece of information from this set of data: the income level of these small landlords. Table 8 sets out the total income data *from all sources*, including rentals, for the total population of clients helped.

Clearly the majority of these small landlords are not high income earners. In 1978-79 over three quarters earned less than $12,000 per annum. In 1980 this had dropped to a little over one in two cases. In 1981-82 and 1982-83 the incidence of cases earning $12,000 or less was roughly one in three (no further drop since 1981-82, but in fact a slight increase). Thus the really poor proportion of small landlords seemed to fall significantly in this five year period, but still constituted a substantial minority of the total.

If one looks at those earning up to $20,000 in the years 1981-82 and 1982-83, the proportions of the total clients are 63.2 percent and 65.3 percent respectively. Thus, in the most recent years for which data are available, only 36.8 percent in 1981-82 and 34.7 percent in 1982-83 (or roughly one in three) of these small landlords earned over $20,070—from all sources.

Table 8: Annual Income Data for all Clients Helped by LSHC

	1978-79 (11 months)		1980		1981-82		1982-83	
	No.	%	No.	%	No.	%	No.	%
Below $4,000	192	22.8	115	9.9	—	—	—	—
$4,000-7,999	221	26.3	178	15.4	—	—	—	—
$8,000-11,999	232	27.6	314	27.1	—	—	—	—
Total $0-11,999	645	76.7	607	52.4	—	—	—	—
$12,000 +	196	23.3	551	47.6	—	—	—	—
To $12,100	—	—	—	—	499	28.7	584	33.0
12,101-14,300	—	—	—	—	205	11.8	174	9.8
14,301-17,200	—	—	—	—	153	8.8	136	7.7
17,201-17,994	—	—	—	—	85	4.9	101	5.7
17,995-20,070	—	—	—	—	159	9.1	161	9.1
Total Up to 20,070	—	—	—	—	1,101	63.2	1,156	65.3
20,070 +	640	36.8	614	34.7	—	—	—	—
Totals	841	100.0	1,158	100.0	1,741	100.0	1,870	100.0

Note: The income data for 1978-79 and 1980 are differently classified from those of 1981-82 and 1982-83 in the original summary records supplied by the LSHC, and the above broken table reflects these classifications. No neater or more explanatory classifications were available from the records given.

Source: LSHC Summary Records, 1978-83.

For purposes of comparison, income statistics are provided in table 9, derived from the 1981 Census of Canada data on the Toronto CMA total population.

It is apparent that in 1980, 52.4 percent of the LSHC clients declared total incomes from all sources of less than $12,000, while census data show that only 13.98 percent of all families in the Toronto CMA had to contend with such a low level of income, 19.84 percent of all private households, 35.57 percent of all males 15 years of age or over (including all those unemployed), and 47.04 percent of the total population 15 years of age and over, regardless of employment status. In fact, the only designated group whose proportion of aggregate incomes less than $12,000 exceeded that of the LSHC client landlords, was that of females of 15 or over, including all those without jobs.

Table 10 may be used to review the small landlord's sources of total income. Referring first to the total column for all years, one reads that one in eight of the 5,625 individual cases was on pension and almost one in ten was unemployed. A further 4.6 percent had only part-time employment. A substantial proportion, almost one in four, reported self-employed status, but it is unclear from the summary records how many of these had jobs other than their small landlording (i.e., did or did not count their landlording as self-employment). The fairly substantial proportion (8.61 percent) of those categorized under "other" employment also goes unexplained, and may be tied in with individual respondents' confusion as to how to treat their small landlording in terms of employment status.

In any case, the largest single employment status group was that of the full-time employed at 41.9 percent for the total period covered. This was almost twice as large as the self-employed group, which was the second largest class. From this, it would appear that a large proportion of these small landlords do have other gainful employment besides their landlording, but despite the income from other sources, their income distribution is still low (as already shown in table 8). One might expect the pensioned, the unemployed, and the part-time employed, making up over 25 percent of this population, to have extremely low incomes. However, from the total income data it is evident that a substantial proportion of the full-time employed clients also earn low total incomes. Almost two-thirds of the total population of clients earned less than $20,000 per year in the last two recorded years, i.e., 1981-82 and 1982-83. Clearly these small landlords are not living off the fat of the land.

Analysis of Problem Areas of Small Landlords Treated at the Centre

In addition to the summaries of client characteristics analysed above, the centre's workload study summary sheets were also made available for the three calendar years 1980, 1981, and 1982. From them, tables 11 and 12 have been

Table 9

Toronto CMA Income Data for 1980

	Families	Private Households	All Males 15+ (incl. unemployed)	All Females 15+ (incl. unemployed)	Males/Females 15+ (incl. unemployed)
Mean Income	$31,238	$28,765	$18,936	$9,831	—
Median Income	$27,775	$25,151	$16,565	$8,346	—
Total Nos.	785,390	1,040,335	1,070,590	788,070	1,858,660
With Income $12K	109,824	206,352	380,762	493,550	874,312
Percent of Group	13.98	19.84	35.57	62.63	47.04

Source: Census of Canada, 1981 Census Tracts, Toronto CMA, cat. no. 95-977, vol 3.

Table 10

Employment Status of LSHC Clients, 1978-83

	1978-79		1980		1981-82		1982-83		Total	
	No.	%	No.	%	No.	%	No.	%	No.	%
Self-employed	143	17.0	312	24.6	431	24.8	418	23.5	1304	23.2
Employed full-time	389	46.3	545	42.9	768	44.2	654	36.9	2356	41.9
Employed part-time	70	8.3	56	4.4	68	3.9	66	3.7	260	4.6
Unemployed	49	5.8	122	9.6	158	9.1	182	10.3	511	9.1
Pensioned	98	11.7	196	15.4	227	13.1	188	10.6	709	12.6
Other	92	10.9	38	3.0	86	4.9	269	15.2	485	8.6
Total	841	100.0	1,269	99.9	1,738	100.0	1,777	100.2	5625	100.0

Source: LSHC Summary Records, 1978-83.

constructed. Table 11 shows the classifications of "problem areas" in which the centre has been involved. A small percentage of the clients processed merely required information (1.8 percent overall), although it is perhaps noteworthy that the number of clients requesting information grew substantially in the three years 1980 to 1982 from 12 to 84—possibly a testimony to the growing reputation of the centre as a helpful service to landlords, even apart from assisting in pressing landlord-tenant problems. However, since the percentage of overall cases is still so small, comments are concentrated on the upper section of the table.

Here it is seen that tenant-related problems constitute the overwhelming majority of the cases treated by the Centre throughout the three year period— overall, some 9 out of 10 of the total of nearly 6,000 cases. Compared to this proportion, the less than 5 percent of cases (286), which deal more with property or with non-tenant-created problems is quite small. Once again, however, one sees a trend downwards in what have been classified as tenant-related problems, and a trend upwards in other types, especially problems concerned with Notice by a Tenant to vacate.

It is possible that problems related to such notices are equally reasonably justified under tenant-related problems as under a more general category; the reason the latter was chosen was that the tenant was ostensibly voluntarily agreeing to vacate, which would indicate the lack of a problem. To the extent that the landlord feels the need for LSHC advice on the matter, however, the agreement/notice may conceal a conflict that goes far deeper (e.g., landlord agrees to waiving rent arrears if tenant signs notice to vacate—tenant then refuses to leave on due date, etc.). Again, lack of case-by-case data leaves one in the position of having to choose categories somewhat arbitrarily, and this has been done in a manner in which it should be difficult to stand justly accused of overstating the case from the statistics available.

Reviewing the categories of tenant-related problems within the total classif- ication, it is evident that three areas make up the bulk of the problems: 1) largest: unpaid rent, or arrears; 2) next: interference with enjoyment/rights, (which might equally be interference with other tenants' rights and enjoyments as those of the landlord—recall Emily Carr's accounts of tenants' complaints about other tenants' noise and disruptive behaviour); and 3) damage to property, (an issue considered important by the ten small landlords personally interviewed, most of whom never considered legal restitution for the damage as practicable for the vast majority of problems). Thus the cases that actually get as far as the LSHC may represent the tip of the iceberg, of the actual arrears, disruptive behaviour, and physical damage experienced day-to-day by landlords. How- ever one speculates, the fact is that these three categories comprised four out of five (79.7 percent) of all the cases treated by the LSHC during the latest three-year period.

Table 11

Categories of Problems Dealt With, as Defined by LSHC

Problems from tenants:	1980 No.	1980 %	1981 No.	1981 %	1982 No.	1982 %	3 Years Combined No.	3 Years Combined %
Arrears of rent	690	47.4	932	44.5	1,081	44.3	2,703	45.1
Persistently late rent	9	0.6	34	1.6	67	2.7	110	1.8
Damage to property	192	13.2	253	12.1	246	10.1	691	11.5
Interference with enjoyment/other rights	387	26.6	522	24.9	473	19.4	1,382	23.1
Mental health problems	6	0.4	47	2.2	56	2.3	112	1.9
Over-crowding	9	0.6	47	2.2	56	2.3	112	1.9
Abandonment	18	1.2	10	0.5	8	0.3	36	0.6
Own occupancy	103	7.1	193	9.2	194	7.9	490	8.2
Small claims court	12	0.8	14	0.7	31	1.3	57	1.0
1. Total problems	1,426	97.9	2,005	95.8	2,156	88.3	5,587	93.2

Table 11: continued

Other rental-related problems:	1980		1981		1982		3 Years Combined	
	No.	%	No.	%	No.	%	No.	%
City work orders or home repair/loan	10	0.7	20	1.0	26	1.1	56	0.9
Rent review	4	0.3	12	0.6	25	1.0	41	0.7
Conversion, renovations, demolition	4	0.3	33	1.6	36	1.5	73	1.2
Agreement/notice by tenant	—	—	9	0.4	107	4.4	116	1.9
2. Total rental-related problems:	18	1.3	74	3.6	194	8.0	286	4.7
Total 1 + 2	1,444	99.2	2,079	99.4	2,350	96.4	5,873	98.0
3. General info	12	0.8	12	0.6	84	3.4	108	1.8
Grand Total	1,456	100.0	2,091	100.0	2,434	98.8	5,981	99.8

Source: LSHC Summary Records, 1980-82.

Who Refers Cases to the Centre?

Attention is now turned to table 12, which provides two sets of data: the total number of client contacts by telephone and personal visit for the three calendar years 1980 to 1982; and the source of client referrals. The second total is far smaller than the first, so one does not know how many of the difference were not referred at all (in which case one wonders how these clients came to hear of the centre), and how many were merely unable or for some reason unwilling to tell who referred them to the centre. Nonetheless, sufficient data are available to provide the base for some meaningful analysis.

The percentage of each category of referral is calculated as a relation to the total number of referrals, rather than to the total number of centre contacts or "total helped." This, as before, errs on the side of caution, providing percentages that in some categories may overstate the degree of referral. The alternative, using "total helped" as a denominator, would in the case of some categories, e.g., the alderman/MP's/MPP's and the police, have resulted in producing some percentages below the level of 0.1 percent, which is the smallest percentage measurement used in the study. It therefore seemed more useful for analysis to adopt the smaller denominator of specifically identified referrals.

As is readily evident from reviewing the overall three year aggregate column, by far the single largest category of referral group was that of friends or former clients. It alone accounted for one in two of the referrals. From this statistic it would appear that the centre is appropriately named as a self-help centre. At the other extreme are the political representatives of all levels—municipal, provincial, and federal. Combined, their overall referrals account for less than one in one hundred of the total. Not far behind the politicians in referral record are the law enforcement officers, those agents of society whose motto is "to serve and protect" (one might legitimately ask whom)—in all they provided a further 1.4 percent of the total referrals. Other social agencies provided better referral service, e.g., the Landlord-Tenant Advisory Bureau and Metro Information, which provided over one in eight of the total referrals, and the sheriff's office, which provided a similar proportion.

The trend as shown over the three year period does not invalidate conclusions that might be drawn from the aggregate data. The largest single contributing group, friends and former clients, grew from 44.7 percent of the total referral in 1980 to 53.2 percent in 1982, and this growth is larger than the growth of any other category. The combined politician's contribution grew explosively in percentage terms, from 0.2 percent in 1980 to 1.2 percent in 1982, but still referred only 22 clients throughout the calendar year of 1982; this represented by far the politicians' best year of service.

Degree of Social Significance of Small Landlords' Problems

Do problems confronted by landlords, be they tenant-related or any other, pose a serious social problem in the aggregate, or do they in reality constitute just a drop in the ocean of total landlord-tenant relations? The reader is again referred to the top section of table 12. During the three-year period from 1980 to 1982, over 31,000 contacts were made between individuals (the vast majority of whom one can reasonably assume were landlords) and the LSHC. Even taking into account some double counting of repeat clients, with repeat cases, this would not appear to represent an insignificant volume of problems encountered by the small landlord population. One, of course, has no way of knowing the total number of problems encountered by the entire population of residential landlords, since many would be ignorant of the LSHC's services or find other channels of remedy, such as consulting their own personal lawyers, bringing actions themselves without legal assistance, or perhaps in the majority of cases, just foregoing the possibility of restitution in the hope that the problem will be resolved without the need for legal recourse.

Yet reference to the separate figures for the three years in table 12 suggests that the incidence of reported problems is growing, and quite significantly, to the extent that the LSHC's volume of business is a good barometer. The LSHC volume grew by 37.8 percent between 1981 and 1982, and by 52.7 percent over the two year period between 1980 and 1982. Other housing academics have suggested that things may in fact be getting better for landlords as a result of Ontario's rent review, or at least that they may enjoy many benefits to offset the problems it caused. For example, in their 1983 study, Miron and Cullingworth assert that, "Landlords have suffered in obvious ways from rent controls, but they have also received real benefits" (p. 71). As evidence for this assertion, which is made both in a universal context and specifically dealing with the effects of rent review in the province of Ontario during the past few years, they cite a U.S. study by Bloomberg as follows:

> The fact is that, despite rent controls, landlords generally have far from suffered. Even at the same rental, net income from property has materially increased because of essentially full occupancy, no cost of acquiring tenants, no collection costs, low turnover, little redecoration and a minimum of repairs and maintenance, curtailment of service and the very important fact that in many communities there had been substantial rent increases before the rent-freeze dates. (Bloomberg 1947, p. 217.)

Noteworthy about this assertion and the citation to support it is that it is based on an analysis of conditions over 35 years out of date, and in no way related to Ontario's rental housing. The LSHC data, which have dealt exclusively with Ontario private rental housing during the more recent years of 1978-83,

Table 12

Sources of Referrals

	1980		1981		1982		3 Years Combined	
Phone calls	4,334		6,017		6,647		16,998	
Drop-ins	3,628		4,952		5,508		14,089	
Total Helped	7,962		10,970		12,155		31,087	

Referred to LSHC by:	No. of clients referred	%	No. of clients referred	%	No. of clients referred	%	No. of clients referred	%
LTAB/Metro Info	172	13.8	204	12.1	—	—	—	—
(Social Agencies)	—	—	—	—	275	15.0	651	13.6
Tel Bk/Media	72	5.8	107	6.3	132	7.2	311	6.5
Police	34	2.7	32	1.9	—	—	66	1.4
Friend/Former Client	558	44.7	830	49.1	978	53.2	2,366	49.5
Sheriff	171	13.7	227	13.4	243	13.2	641	13.4
Others	239	19.1	278	16.4	189	10.3	706	14.8
Alderman/MP/MPP	3	0.2	12	0.7	22	1.2	37	0.8
Don't know/no referral	?	?	?	?	?	?	?	?
Total known referral sources	1,249	100.0	1,690	99.9	1,839	100.1	4,778	100.0

Source: LSHC Summary Records, 1980-82.

have shown no evidence to support a diminution of problems or "suffering" for the thousands of private landlords comprising its client population.

If it is suggested that landlords suffer no more than other business people, then the facts have not been fully taken into consideration. Since 1975 most private landlords have had their gross income severely restricted by legislation. This has been imposed on no other section of private business. The effect has not just been to restrict gross and net incomes, but through the capitalization effect, to reduce the value of the capital assets (Laverty 1982). This in turn has restricted the marketability of rental properties, so that at the meetings of landlords the frequent complaint is made that they would love to sell their properties and get out of the business but are unable to find a buyer. (See detailed comments of survey questionnaires distributed in Toronto, reproduced in appendix B.) Again, this type of "suffering" has been created by the landlord-tenant legislation, and is different from the suffering of other businessmen. Finally, landlord-tenant legislation has granted increasingly long-term rights to tenants. This tends to create a long-term relationship between tenant and landlord, whether either likes it or not. Most business people have freedom to service customers or not, and the only cost to them is loss of trade. The landlord has far less freedom of choice. In short, it would be difficult to identify the situation of the landlord with that of other business people who may terminate client-induced suffering at their own discretion.

Further study would be required to determine whether rent review has made landlords economically better off. Although one might suspect the reverse, the data supplied by the LSHC and analysed here could neither support nor refute such a contention. A complementary study (Lehrer 1984A) therefore uses different, though secondary, data to deal with overall economic trends.

Statistical Qualifications and General Conclusions

A couple of concluding comments to the study of the LSHC records are in order. First, they should not be taken as necessarily representative of all landlords' experiences. It would be reasonable to assume that the larger the landlord, the less the chance that he would need to avail himself of the LSHC's services because of his technical landlording knowledge already acquired through large-scale experience, and his presumed greater ability to pay for specialized and professional service, such as legal advice, etc., when tenant and landlording problems arose. For these reasons and others then, throughout the study the belief is stressed that the great majority if not all of the LSHC's clients can be considered to consist of relatively "small" landlords.

Whether the LSHC client population can be taken as reasonably representative of all small landlords is a more difficult question to answer. The large number of clients processed in the years reviewed (over 14,000 referrals, roughly 5,600 cases) would naturally increase the statistical claims of representation. But these might be somewhat invalidated, or at any rate lessened by the possibility that the sample is neither randomly selected among small landlords, nor pre-stratified. In other words, it could be argued that as tenant legal aid clinics, etc., tend to represent poor, underprivileged tenants, creating a biased sample with which to represent the total population of tenants, so the Landlord Self-Help Centre, located as it is in a poor section of Toronto, would tend to attract as clients an overlarge proportion of poor and underprivileged landlords, and possibly an over-representation of ethnic minority groups, which would create bias in any sample used on the basis of it that claimed to represent the total small landlord population.

There may be some truth to this argument. On the other hand, it is also increasingly likely that, as the LSHC has become better known, an increasing number of its clients have come to the centre from dispersed areas. Some clients do already come from outside the Metro area. If there is nowhere else for small landlords to go for inexpensive and sympathetic assistance, the centre's geographic location may affect the representative quality of its clientele very little. Moreover, it is also possible to argue, to the extent that the returns to small-time landlording have become increasingly suspect as we witness in Ontario some degree of repetition of the U.K. experience well described in Eversley's "Landlord's Slow Goodbye" (New Society, 1975), that the majority of small landlords remaining who have not managed to sell out to a large operation or to a private homeowner (who will convert the rental units [back] to homeownership) will tend to be the poorer, less privileged individuals, many of whom are already represented in our LSHC population.

Survey Lacunae

One might note that according to P. Laverty of the Ontario Ministry of Municipal Affairs and Housing in a (1983) telephone discussion, no comprehensive statistics exist on the number and holdings of private-sector landlords in Ontario. The Ontario Government Green Paper (1978) stated that according to its 1974 survey of housing units there were some 38,000 live-in landlords. If one assumes that the 1974 number has not dwindled substantially as small landlords have sold off their holdings and left the business, then one might expect the total number of private-sector residential landlords to be in the range of 40,000 to 60,000 in Ontario, the vast majority of whom could be reasonably defined as small landlords.

In his Boston study, *The Other Bostonians—Poverty and Progress in the American Metropolis, 1880-1970*, Thernstrom found the same difficulty of identifying the population of private landlords as has been found in Toronto. Under occupational rankings (p. 290) he classifies builders and contractors with sufficient property as major proprietors, etc. He explains in a note that "sufficient property" was defined as $5,000 in real estate. He continues,

> The arbitrary cut-off point may seem low,...but I was more interested in keeping a reasonable homogeneity of status in the petty proprietor than in the large proprietor category. In any event the available information about property holdings as explained previously, was scanty for the later samples and absent altogether for that drawn from the 1958 city directory...(p. 292.)

Chapman noted the same difficulty of landlord reticence in his (1981) Auckland Ph.D. study of the private rental/ownership market. The CMHC has advised that it has not undertaken a comprehensive landlord study, showing such things as income, etc. This present study is therefore not alone in having encountered difficulties in identifying parameters for the total residential landlord population.

Thus, while it is true that the LSHC analysis cannot claim 100 percent representability of the total small landlord population, in the absence of better data, it may serve as a guide. The next stage would be a more comprehensive and statistically representative landlord sample, including from the private sector small, intermediate, and large landlords organized on a personal, private corporate, and public corporate basis. For completeness, one might also want to include social housing and public housing landlords in such a study, since non-profit sector housing may be destined to take over an increasingly larger share of the total rental housing sector. Such research would provide more complete analysis, but would be costly, time-consuming, and extremely difficult in terms of data capture, and is therefore considered far beyond the bounds of this more modest one-person study.

CHAPTER 6

Small Scale Landlording as an Occupation

Focusing exclusively on analysing data that relates only to problems may tend to make one lose sight of the fact that landlording is an occupation, like teaching, nursing, and plumbing, and therefore has a claim to be studied under the heading of occupations (Hughes 1971). This has been confounded by the fact that landlord-tenant relations are often compared to industrial relations, thus putting the landlord (rightly or wrongly) in a position analogous to that of employer or boss (e.g., Donnison 1967). The final section of this chapter is therefore spent attempting to shed some light on these two different approaches to landlording, both of which are closely related to the issue of power.

Alan Fox, in a 1974 work focused mainly on the development of labour relations, talks of a fundamental change in the nature of human relations that has to do with work. He compares a basically social exchange in pre-industrial society, where loyalties, activities, and responsibilities were quite diffuse, to the situation since the industrial revolution characterized by an economic exchange, where transactions of all sorts are reduced to the impersonal common denominator of *how much is it worth?* Contract is the epitome of this economic exchange. It represents the short-term nature of the relations (lasting only the duration of the contract) and characterizes the fundamental lack of trust between the parties. Of course in the case of landlords and tenants, the economic contract is manifested specifically in the written (and often highly protective and complex) lease agreement.

Fox's idea that the economic contract underlines the lack of trust between parties is worth extrapolating to the area of landlord-tenant relations, which may often be marked by mutual hostility and mistrust if not downright suspicion. The landlord has often been referred to with the introductory epithet "slum," and with an image as tainted as a pariah, he has come to be compared to pimps, prostitutes, and other social outcasts whose "vile bodies we should love" (Lubbock 1977). He therefore has much social prejudice to combat from the outset. He can adopt different strategies to minimize his suffering from this phenomenon. The particular strategy adopted will depend, 1) on whether he is part-time or full-time, small-scale or large-scale, live-in or absentee; and 2) whether he is more interested in economic optimizing or in minimizing social discomfort (the two considerations are not mutually independent).

It has already been stated that the strategy adopted by landlords belonging to ethnic minorities may be to try to choose tenants from their own community, not just from a sense of social obligation but also to protect themselves from the implications of a purely economic exchange. Thus, a diffuseness of responsibilities may enter into the contractual relationship, to borrow from Fox's terms. A relationship far more trusting than the general run of landlord-tenant relationships may then evolve for the benefit of both parties, but especially for the landlord.

However, in the more common case, the landlord does not rent exclusively to his own ethnic group. Is the landlord then trapped in a social role not of his own making but which is nonetheless inescapable? Goffman (1959), writing exhaustively on roles and the necessity of masks, shows how, in an increasingly task-specialized world, audiences come to rely on particular modes of role-playing (the plumber on the job takes off his glasses to act out the role of looking tough, etc.). If the audiences do not receive the act they expect, they are either disappointed, let down in some way, or confused.

Division of Labour

Many of the significant authors throughout the short history of sociology (Durkheim 1947, Weber 1946, Bell 1973) have dwelt on the increasing division of labour as an important phenomenon. The recent concern has been with the attempts to professionalize jobs in order to prove their financial worth in an increasingly competitive and status-conscious society and to improve their image, not necessarily just for financial reasons but for more compelling reasons of social prestige (Lehrer 1980B, 1981B).

How does landlording fit into this analysis? Like a fish swimming against the stream. The small landlord, with whom this analysis has been mostly concerned, must in fact serve many functions and thus is forced to fulfil many roles. This tends to de-professionalize and thereby tarnish his image, as if his image were not already discoloured enough. Not only does he have to act as bill collector but unless he is quite well off, he will have to fulfil at least some of the functions of janitor—garbage collection, cleaning windows, washing floorways, putting on and taking off storm windows, and other more or less menial and dirty jobs. As Hughes (1971) points out in his discussion of doctors and nurses, the medical and other similarly prestigious professionals conceal their dirty and menial tasks, physically where feasible or by giving them portentous labels. (A surgeon "performs an operation," rather than covering himself with a bloody mess.) Best of all, they may be able to push the dirty, unglamorous, "unprofessional" tasks down a rung to a different occupational niche (nursing aides in this context become very convenient).

A landlord, as opposed to a doctor, can only perform the same sleight of hand by making it plain to tenants that his functions are delineated quite rigorously. Thus he is entitled to the respect due a property owner (a "lord of the land"), whilst the menial tasks are the sole responsibility of an appointee, optimally a permanent, full-time factotum superintendent. From this vantage point, not only can the landlord regain some of his "backstage" but he can also adopt the role of arbiter or quasi-high court judge in cases of conflict between tenants and super.

Even this role is not a heavenly one. It still requires time and energy dealing with the endless stream of complaints about the inefficiency, laziness, and dishonesty of the super (most supers, as every tenant knows, have the above qualities). But from the landlord's point of view, the arbiter's role is infinitely preferable to being first on the firing line. It gives him a much-needed buffer-cum-whipping-boy, and provides him with a less diverse, less confused, and more prestigious if not quite a professional status. Superintendents and property managers might be available to the more successful intermediate landlord, and they would be essential to a large-scale operator, but this strategy would not normally be economically available to the type of small landlord represented by Emily Carr, by the ten landlords I interviewed, or by the clients at LSHC. The differences in the strategy options available to each classification of landlord represent a good reflection of the strength of their relative power bases.

There are other elements of strategy that a relatively small landlord may adopt towards his tenants. One may talk in Fred Fiedler's (1967) terms of a contingency model similar to leadership models in manager-subordinate relations. The structural variables would be the type of landlord—part-time, full-time, live-in, absentee, etc.—but personality factors would also enter the picture. Does the landlord see himself as an out-going personable type? Does he enjoy socializing? Is he interested mostly in maintaining a professional front? Both of these sets of factors will tend to determine where the landlord will seek to identify himself along the continuum of personal-impersonal relations with tenants.

Necessarily, the relationship is also determined to some degree by the other party, the tenant, so that the landlord's strategy is restricted to what is acceptable to tenants, just as the manager's strategy options are limited by subordinate behaviour and perceptions. In many cases, the tenant's image of the landlord is very negative, and will therefore make a strategy of warm personal relations quite difficult to pursue. On the other hand some tenants may simply refuse to accept formal landlord-tenant roles and may want to enjoy a warm personal relationship with their landlord. Once again, Emily Carr's experiences are referred to for illustration, not all of which were bitter: She writes,

I was making my garden when they came to live in my house. They would come rushing down the stair, he to seize my spade, she to play the hose so that I could sit and rest a little. They shared their jokes and giggles with me.

When at dusk, aching and tired, I climbed to my flat, on my table was napkin and plate with a little surprise whose odor was twin to that of the supper in the Doll's House [the tenants' flat].

Sometimes...when things were bothersome, difficult, so that I just hated being a landlady, she would pop a merry joke or run an arm around me, or he would say "Shall I fix that leak?—put up that shelf?"

Oh, they were like sunshine pouring upon things... (op. cit., pp. 31-32.)

Taking Advantage

There are problems with such warm interludes of good interpersonal relations between landlord and tenant. First, the softening process will tend to make the landlord that much more vulnerable and gullible for the next group of tenants who will be able to take advantage of such weakness. Second, the majority of even the originally good tenants will not turn out to be saints. The landlord will find himself emotionally torn in the event of (more or less inevitable) conflict situations, such as technical breakdowns, NSF cheques, rent increases, etc. At that point the "personal relations" may be turned by the tenant into a strategy of demanding from the landlord more privileges than those to which he is legally entitled or, from the landlord's viewpoint, to which the tenant is morally entitled on the basis of the relationship that has been established.

The strategy of personal relations may appear initially to help and suit the landlord. However, rather than promoting trust and a diffuse notion of mutual responsibilities (as Fox theorizes is the optimal situation in employer-employee relations), personal relationships may instead end up by being a far more exploitable strategy for the tenant than the landlord. It is arguable that exploitation may cut both ways, but for "good behaviour" or the sake of peaceful relations, tenants may be able to buy some substantial material and financial benefits. The potential for some degree of moral blackmail would thus appear to favour the tenant, thus making good relations less than reciprocal in their actual costs and benefits.

The final word on small landlord strategy should be allowed to Emily Carr since she formed the introduction to chapter 3 and has acted to some degree as a touchstone throughout. She writes, "It took a long time to grind me into the texture of a landlady, to level my temperament, to make it neither all up nor all down." (op. cit. p. 13.)

In short, the long-term survival of a small landlord might appear to require emotional separation, a lack of involvement with tenants in any meaningful sense, and possibly establishing a miniature bureaucratic apparatus to protect all parties from psychological realities and help maintain the sanity of the landlord. Such strategies are of course inimical to warm social relations and can only promote a society filled with the degenerative malaise of anomy. Berger (1967) maintained that human beings must remain social beings and therefore socially acceptable in order to sustain the motivation to survive. If this is accepted, one may find here a further strong socio-psychological reason for the gradual demise of the small private landlord, especially among the favoured segments of the population. Since the psychological benefits may be considered either negligible or negative, only those with little choice may take up the occupation—e.g., members of minority groups who do not yet perceive themselves in a position to afford the luxury of avoiding situations with low or negative emotional rewards. Marxist analysis of alienation may end up explaining the position of small landlords in our "democratic" society better than it does the role of organized labour!

CHAPTER 7

Summary

This study has been chiefly concerned with the nature and workings of power in society. It has used the housing sub-system of society for this purpose, and has attempted to show how the private rental sector of housing reflects and is dependent upon the major institutions on which the whole of society is based. It has argued that the commonly discussed institutions making up the social structure—the economic framework, political and governmental bodies, media and educational institutions, etc.—all have one grounding element in common that gives them societal significance: power.

The phenomenon of social power has been explored. For the purposes of examining the effect of societal power on a sub-system such as housing, aggregate power was split into its relevant constituent elements, or power bases. These were then used as a framework within which to analyse the relative power positions of some of the various major actors in the private housing scene. The analysis pointed to the relative stability of some actors, e.g., homeowners, and the relative state of flux in the power positions of others, notably private tenants and landlords. This was related to a number of factors: the changing concept of property in society, the intervention of governmental power, and the ideals of democracy with its far more questionable practical functioning. In specific terms, the rule of the majority has in private rental housing produced an oppression of the less powerful minority groups in society.

This theme of oppression of the powerless, made covert by the democratic process, has been associated mostly with the ethnic status of the powerless actor. It has been traced through the small landlord community and the private tenant population. Many of society's power brokers have resorted to the justifying ideology of social democracy, sometimes with anti-capitalist and Marxist overtones but by no means always. This includes politicians, much of the media, academics, etc., most of whom have an ethnic background in common with the majority group in the democratic State, and whose social construction of reality may therefore be set along conventional class lines. Such a supportive framework of power and its handmaiden ideology have helped even more those actors in the housing sector who have openly espoused the ideology, in the form of participatory non-profit housing such as housing co-operatives.

The composition of political representation at the provincial level and of coercive institutions of government were found to reflect and buttress the power distribution among ethnic groups found in the housing sub-system, again regardless of ideological distinctions such as the capitalism of the landlord, the assumed non-capitalism of the tenant, or the anti-capitalist non-profit orientation expected of the co-op housing member.

Yet the power differentials of actors and institutions change over time, not by the realignment of different alliances or the intentional amassing and deployment of additional arsenals of power but by changes in the value framework of society. This changes the perceived societal value of the combination of power bases held by different actors and institutions. Thus, the role of those with access to manipulating and re-formulating a society's values— teaching and religious personnel and institutions, political and judicial actors and institutions, the media and its personnel, etc.,—in aggregate hold awesome responsibility for the ultimate repository of societal power. How well they collectively meet their responsibilities can be measured in part by the distribution of power among society's actors. In the context of this study, the actual as opposed to the assumed power in aggregate societal terms of the small private landlord is the focal point.

Tenant Abuses of Rent Control Systems

Recently in New York some publicity has attached to extremely wealthy and famous people who, because of rent controls, have lived for years in huge downtown suites at negligible rents. An amusing case the author knows of is one where a couple "own" a rent-controlled suite, i.e., have rented it for decades and regard it as their own. They are millionaires in the diamond business and spend most of their time, when not travelling in Europe, at their California home where their Rolls Royce is well known. Their daughter hit the nail on the head: it's far cheaper keeping the apartment for use the odd couple of days a month than resorting to a downtown hotel!

As always, Toronto follows New York as fast as it can. Our rent control system now makes it highly profitable for the wealthy business owner to stay renting his large Harbourside suite, rather than purchasing it at a cost approaching $1 million. A more inventive abuse of the system has been perpetrated by two downtown lawyers. One sold her condominium for $250 thousand, on the condition of a one-year leaseback, and providing a one year mortgage. A year later she (quite legally) demanded mortgage repayment or a far higher interest rate for renewal and, at the same time, refused to move out on the grounds that it was her home! She advised the purchasers that in her legal experience no judge would evict her as a tenant on the grounds of the landlord wanting it as his own home. Again, the tenant was a millionaire, already owning several suites in the Harbourside complex.

A final case worthy of note is that of another lawyer who had been renting in the Yonge-Eglinton area of high-rise, low-cost rent-controlled apartment buildings. (Typical rent of a two bedroom in the 110-140-160 Erskine complex in Toronto in 1988 is $500 to $600 per month, about half its current market value.) He had decided to upgrade, had purchased the downtown building of his thriving legal practice, and rather than give up the highly subsidized rent-controlled apartment, he was sub-letting it and still enjoying all the extensive facilities of the complex (squash, sauna, indoor pool, tennis, etc.).

Other tenants openly advertise their apartments as available, but give up their rights to "the property" in return for a lump sum paid by the incoming tenant. The "key money" is often disguised as payment for furnishings or fixtures. An economist might describe it as the cost of an annuity of the difference between rent-controlled and market rent. An incoming tenant justifiably regards it as exploitation of a monopoly situation by the more fortunate vacating tenant.

The above disparate cases all have one thing in common: they have been made possible by the creation of an artificial system that creates an ever-increasing unsatisfied demand for a limited number of "goodies." The conventional economic arguments against rent control are well known and need not be reproduced here (see Block & Olson 1981). What has been less extensively examined is the demographic profile of the fortunate, subsidized tenants, compared to those paying rents set close to market value. As the system becomes more permanently entrenched, an elite class of tenants who have the most subsidized units will be created. These rental units will not necessarily be the cheapest, but will be the most desirable in terms of location and space, e.g., Yonge-Eglinton and High Park in Toronto. The elite residents may then choose to enjoy their subsidized rental space or "sell" it in any of the ways described above or in others. The more knowledgeable and richer tenants will be able to turn the situation to their greatest advantage. As generations pass, the possibly random original distribution of tenants living in the most heavily subsidized rental units will have been replaced by those tenants who have been able and willing to buy the on-going subsidy from the original occupants.

Abstracting, then, from the moral issue of wealthy tenants making (untaxed?) capital profits out of the rental system, the basic social and political issues remain. Who ultimately benefits most from a permanent infrastructure of rent controls? If the cases above represent the tip of the iceberg of legal rent control abuse by tenants, it is no wonder that governments prefer to continue stating platitudes about helping "poor tenants" and moderate income groups through rent controls. The alternative—examining the actual demographics of the most subsidized renters—would be too politically embarrassing. If tenant political power was originally based on numbers, the abuses facilitated by rent control systems will increasingly add to the number of wealthy and professional tenants. As new elements of power strengthen the power base of the tenant population, we may expect their political voice to be even more firmly entrenched and legitimated. As at the end of Orwell's *Animal Farm* a new meaning for the word "equal" had been created, so in our time a new meaning for the phrase "rent power" will have evolved for successive generations.

APPENDIX A

Summary Questionnaire Distributed to 100 Ontario Residential Landlords, with its Accompanying Letter

June 29, 1983

Dear Sir/Madam:

A number of researchers have complained about the lack of available information relating to landlords, especially with regard to the Ontario landlords' experiences during the past seven years of rent controls. Some have, therefore, made assumptions in the absence of evidence to the contrary which may not reflect the reality of the landlords' financial, social, and personal experience in conducting his rental operations.

In an effort to rectify this lack of information, it would be of great help if you would complete the following two questionnaires of your own experiences of rental operations during the past 10 years.

The first questionnaire is short. It would be much appreciated if you would complete and return it here immediately. The second requires financial and other data which you may not have immediately available. However, your effort in researching the data, as far as possible, from your past records would provide a significant contribution to the knowledge of the conditions under which residential rental landlords have been operating in Ontario. Your help and co-operation will be much appreciated.

Please send the second completed questionnaire to:

> Professor Keith Lehrer
> 11 Munro Park Avenue
> Toronto, Ontario
> M4E 3M2

N.B. YOUR NAME AND ADDRESS ARE NOT REQUIRED ON THE QUESTIONNAIRE.

Ontario Residential Landlords' Summary Questionnaire

1. How many years have you owned residential rental property in Ontario?
   _____

2a. How many residential rental units do you own? _____

2b. How many did you own in 1975? _____

3. Do you live in a unit in your own building? _____

4. Which age range do you fall into:

   Under 25___   25-34___   35-44___   45-54___   55-64___   65___

5. What is your marital status?

   Single___   Married___   Widowed___   Divorced/Separated___

6. Relationship and age of any dependants?

   1.

   2.

   3.

   4.

   5.

   6.

   More than 6

7. For which years, if any, have you applied for a rent increase above the guideline?

	1976	1977	1978	1979	1980	1981	1982
percent increase applied for							
percent increase obtained							

8. If you have been in operation for eight years or more, have you experienced better ____, worse ____, or similar ____ relations in general with your tenants since 1976?

9. Have you experienced more ____ less ____ a similar ____ amount of minor damage and vandalism performed by tenants since 1976?

10. Have you experienced more ____ less ____ a similar ____ amount of major damage and vandalism performed by tenants since 1976?

11. Have your maintenance expenditures increased ____ decreased _____ stayed about the same ____ since 1976?

12. To the extent that you are able to control maintenance and repair expenditures, (i.e., apart from emergency and essential expenditures) do you plan in the future to increase expenditures ____ decrease ____ or maintain them at about the same level ____ in the long-term future?

13. What was the first language of your childhood? _____

14a. What was your mothers's first language _____

your father's first language _____

14b. What ethnic group do you consider you belong to? _____

15. How many times, and in what years, have you approached your local alderman, MPP, or MP for advice/assistance on problems related to your residential rental property?

16. In general, what was their response?
Extremely helpful ___ Helpful ___ Unhelpful ___ Extremely unhelpful ___
Other (please specify...)

17. What are your principal reasons for keeping your residential rental property?
 i)
 ii)
 iii)
 iv)
 v)

18. In what bracket did your rental income/loss fall during the past nine years, ignoring tax payments and allowances?

Net Loss from rental

	$100,000 or more	$50,000 to 99,999	$25,000 to 49,999	$15,000 to 24,999	$5,000 to 14,999	$1 to 4,999
1982						
1981						
1980						
1979						
1978						
1977						
1976						
1975						
1974						

Net Income from rentals

	$0 to 4,999	$5,000 to 14,999	$15,000 to 24,999	$25,000 to 49,999	$50,000 to 99,999	$100,000 or more
1982						
1981						
1980						
1979						
1978						
1977						
1976						
1975						
1974						

19. Apart from your rental operation, are you otherwise employed or self-employed?

Yes ___   No ___   Part-time ___   Full-time ___

20. In what bracket did your total income fall for the same years?

1982	
1981	
1980	
1979	
1978	
1977	
1976	
1975	
1974	

Thank you very much for completing this questionnaire.
If you have any further comments, please feel free to add them here:

APPENDIX B

Detailed Comments of Ontario Landlords in Questionnaire Responses—Verbatim

1. We are following Europe's footsteps, in that Canada is turning more socialistic, supporting the working poor, i.e., tenants. They get all the advantages and breaks, whilst the small landlord, who has to work extremely hard just to hold on to what he has worked so hard for, is considered the bad guy. Trudeau's socialist government is making sure that fewer people are willing to work hard in order to make small profits and provide others with adequate housing, to the point where only fools would invest in income properties!

    As for rent-review: it is totally inadequate. Who can afford the time and expenditure to document the ever so necessary above 6 percent rent increases? Most small landlords have full-time jobs and can ill afford taking lots of time off—it's a never-ending procedure, totally useless!!!

    As for rent-control: it's totally outdated, unnecessary, and to the detriment of both the landlord and the tenant. With shopping inflation and rising expenditures, the 6 percent ceiling is absolutely insane!!!

2. The remedies available to landlords for non payment are ludicrous. Small claims grants a judgement after your incurring the costs but you haven't got a hope in hell of collecting on it.

3. Rent control as it is now is not just—not fair—no good.

4. I don't want to be a landlord!

5. Rent controls are contributory to future slums.

6. Why Small Segment of older Building Only Keeping under rent Control Only, but not Total industry and everything else? Why Small Landlord must Suffer unbearable Condition of rent Control? Provincial *Government offering help for Small Business* (financial), but for Small Landlord putting pressure. Where are justice? My former tenants 7 (seven) of them bought houses, one of them bought triplex. They are in better position than myself. They are able much more Safe money due to favourable Condition of rent Control (protection). They are able to go for trips outside Canada. But I am Working like Slave. When provincial government Wake up? Or [do they] Want to destroy private enterprise?

7. Rent control is absolutely impossible. It is socialistic, degrading, demoralizing, and just impossible to deal with. I am seriously considering selling just because of rent control but may wait for these commission findings—I just hope it won't get worse.

    I cannot complete questionnaire on Ontario residential landlords detailed in Questionnaire—I do not keep files as detailed as you ask there.

8. The landlords are being forced out of the private sector because of rent controls. A survey of the average age of a landlord is about 50 years old.

Therefore, the scenario we are faced with is 1) apartments operated by the government 2) apartment conversions.

9. Poor tenants should be supported through the public at large and not by small owners of rental properties.

    The government should buy apartment buildings at fair market value and rent the units as it pleases, similar to public housing.

    The shortage for apartment space has been influenced by changes in social behaviour. An increase in the number of families splitting up due to separation or divorce causes a doubling in demand for accommodation.

    Similarly the trend for children to move into their own apartment at an earlier age also increases the demand for housing.

    Those causing the additional demand should be made responsible for the cost. Hardship help has to come from public funds and not from small apartment building owners, etc.

10. I generally feel that Ontario government has been very unfair to the small landlord, has undermined the business in every sense, and shows a complete lack of responsibility in that the landlord is forced to subsidize his tenants and cannot claim legitimate expenses.

    Landlord/Tenant relations are deteriorating day by day and some tenants are getting vicious and demanding as a result.

11. We don't really have problems but considering the value of the three properties (five units) our income is no where near what we would earn if we invested similar moneys in other ways. This is really not fair.

12. In our case, ethnic background plays no role.

    I can only stress that in order to survive financially, our own free unpaid labour is required. This is an enormous strain. I had to work to subsidize tenants, instead of being at home with our three small children. As my husband bitterly says, "Every one of our tenants has a better quality of life than we."

    Between salaried job and unpaid landlording, my husband used to work 100 hours per week.

    Between salaried job (money going to pay building's expenses), unpaid landlording, and barely looking after household and family, I worked 100 hours per week. We have pulled back somewhat this last year. My husband works perhaps 60 hours per week. I have stopped my salaried job, but work full time at landlording (no pay) to help relieve my husband. The lack of my salary has meant that we have not been keeping up with property tax payments. On one property, realty tax A/P stands now at less than $20,000.

    We cannot raise rents higher than they are, since all around our building other buildings charge considerably less than we do (owners with low mortgages, holding property already 20 to 30 years). These owners sit on a lot of equity for which they get no earnings. They cannot justify higher rents to the commission. So we feel the squeeze between controls and market competition.

13. The best tenants are immigrants and the best tenants by far are Chinese immigrants.

14. Because of rent control and the free access of tenants to inspectors, Legal Aid, etc., the landlord has been made the scapegoat for the government. We do not have organizations booking up against undercared tenants—our machinery is very small. My building is up for sale and I can't sell it because nobody wants to subsidize tenants. However the Government wants to buy it for co-operative housing and is squeezing out the "entrepreneurs" and small landlords. At this point, I'm negotiating with them and they are slowly conditioning me to sell at their price—*socialism* not *free* enterprise.

15. We have been renting to adults only for a year or so because we find the tenants feel their children have a right to do as they please and most tenants deny all responsibility for their children.

When children have done considerable damage and I go to the rent board to evict them, the rent board tells they must stop the vandalism and then dismisses the case and leaves you with the tenant laughing at you. With the present attitude of rent boards we are powerless to control tenants as along as they pay the rent!

Comments by Toronto and Ontario Politicians on Tenants' Rights, Landlords' Rights, and Rent Review

Note the consistency of view among politicians from ostensibly diverse party political backgrounds. The question-response summary excerpted from the *Globe and Mail* provides an apposite illustration.

WHERE THE PARTIES STAND
Responses to questions posed by The Globe and Mail on key issues
(18 March 1981)
Question: Some argue that rent controls are partly to blame for the current rental housing shortage. Would your party maintain rental controls? What would your party do to deal with the rental housing shortage?

Conservatives

We recently made a clear commitment to continuing rent review as a permanent program. Even without rent review, rental production would be low, given high interest rates.

Under the new $63-million Ontario Rental Construction Loan Program 15,000 units will be built in 1981.

The province also supports municipal non-profit housing and has provided additional incentives to federally administered private non-profit and co-operative housing groups.

Liberals

We are firmly committed to maintaining the 6 percent limit on annual rent increases. To get construction of moderate-income rental units under way again, our Rental Housing Incentive Plan offers mortgages to builders at 25 percent below market rates. The money will be raised by selling five-year Ontario housing bonds to the public. This program should stimulate 30,000 new rental housing starts over the next five years.

New Democrats

We are pressing the Conservatives to retain rent controls and we plan to extend controls to buildings occupied since the end of 1975 and to close other loopholes in the present system.

The high interest-rate policy of the federal and provincial governments is the prime cause of the housing construction slowdown, not rent controls.

New Democrats believe that housing is a social right. In addition to strengthening rent controls to protect tenants we would greatly increase the provision of co-operative and non-profit housing.

APPENDIX D

Ethic Minority Landlords in Auckland, New Zealand*

Ethnicity Among Landlords

Research by Krohn et al. (1979) in Montreal, Canada, and by Rex and Moore (1967) in the suburbs of Birmingham, England, suggest that a high proportion of landlords belong to ethnic minority groups, and Rex goes on to analyze how they are encouraged by the host society to take that role because it has a pariah status. Thus the host society gets an essential function fulfilled, but can still abuse those providing the service because those fulfilling it are social outcasts anyway.

The results of this present study do not confirm that there is a preponderance of ethnic minority individuals in landlord roles in the Auckland region. On the contrary the great majority (89.8 percent) indicated that they did not belong to minority ethnic groups. However, the proportion (10.2 percent) of respondents who did report belonging to an ethnic minority (none of them Maori or Pacific Island Polynesian) is worth comparing to the statistics on non-Maori and non-Polynesian ethnic minorities reported in the 1983 New Zealand Official Year Book.

The sub-total of other ethnic groups, including Chinese, Indian, Fijian, Syrian, Lebanese, Arab, and others is 42,219 in the Year Book. Although Jews are not included as an ethnic minority in the Year Book classification, they are included as a separate religious group under "Hebrew Congregational" in the religious classification of the population. For purposes of this study it would seem appropriate to include them along ethnic minority groups, thus adding 3,360 to the 42,219 making 45,579 in all. This represents 1.45 percent of the total New Zealand population, compared to the 10.2 percent of landlord respondents who reported ethnic minority status (some seven times greater). As discussed in chapter 2 [of the Auckland research study], we have reason to believe that the reporting of ethnic minority status may under-represent the actual proportion of respondents who belong to ethnic minority groups.

Interview

Among the landlords personally interviewed at least six out of twenty belonged to an ethnic minority group. Others had mixed parentage and the ethnic status of others was not known. However, the interviewers were not randomly chosen, and it would therefore be completely incorrect to draw inferences from their far higher representation of minority ethnic status.

*This is reprinted from "A Profile of the Private Residential Landlord in Auckland, and His Role in Rental Housing," Lehrer, 1984, chapter 4.

In order to shed light on some of the experiences of the ethnic minorities in landlording, an attempt was made to contact two of the Asian communities known to have landlords. The information provided by one of them, the Indian community, is considered sufficiently valid to warrant reporting in the study.

The physician whose interview was reported among the personal interviews provided the contacts with other members of the Indian community in Auckland. The first interviewed, Mr. N., was a justice of the peace and not a landlord. He owns his own home, but rents his dairy premises. In addition to running his dairy with five other members of his family, he works part-time for the post office.

Mr. N. explained that the Indian community was close-knit, and members of the family and extended family were expected to help each other, and did so. Thus, in finding funds to purchase their own home, which had a high priority for reasons of security among the community, friends and relatives would help each other. The normal convention was to provide one's children, where possible, with sufficient funds for them to make their deposit on their first home.

Family Orientation

Mr. N. estimated there were about 500 families in the Auckland Indian community. The immigration process had been different here than in the U.K., in so far as it had been highly controlled and very gradual. Most of the immigrants had to be relatively self-sufficient as a precondition for entry, and could rely on the support system of the cohesive community already established.

Mr. N. felt that many among the Indian community were now conscious that being full-time residential landlords would "degrade their name," so most had avoided it as a full-time business. For illustration he cited his uncle who used to be a residential landlord, but eventually gave up his operation—he was unable to obtain the rent regularly from his tenants, and there was a great deal of damage and theft. Consequently many among the community had switched to commercial property, where relationships with tenants were less stressful, there was less chance of the tenants walking out and not paying rent, and they were responsible for some of the expenses such as rates.

The other member of the Indian community interviewed, Mr. P., is a lawyer who represents the legal affairs of many families in the Indian community, and therefore had good "inside" knowledge of the community's involvement in private rental housing. He estimated that, although the first investment priority of his clients was to own the premises of their own dairy, still some 150 to 200 families in the community have an extra house in addition to their principal family residence. Often it was the first house that the family had owned, which they had not sold when buying their second. The first was often kept as "insurance" of a roof over the heads of the next generation. Meanwhile, it was rented. An estimated 30-50 percent were used to house members of their own community who had not yet bought their own homes.

Insurance

Mr. P. does not recommend the retention of the first house to his clients, since it often turns out to create so many problems. Many of his clients complain to him about not getting their rent and having bad relationships with their tenants. Mr. P. tells them they should consider themselves fortunate if the tenant vacates voluntarily after a month's non-payment and some property damage.

Going through due process of law for eviction would be far more wearing and costly for his clients. He feels some of the bad relationships are due to the resentment tenants feel about having a "foreigner" as their landlord. For all these reasons, Mr. P. does not encourage his clients to become residential landlords. In fact, many are currently trying to get out of the business to avoid problems with the TPA, Health Department, etc. Due primarily to the rise in mortgage interest rates coupled with controlled rents, the economics of residential landlording make no sense either, according to Mr. P.

The overall impression left from these interviews with representatives from visible minority ethnic groups active in rental housing is similar to Rex's analysis of the U.K., but the exigencies of population density and a tough economic situation have been attenuated in New Zealand compared to the U.K. for such ethnic minorities. This would appear to have left them far more in control of their own destinies, and they have recently been increasingly opting to get out of the residential rental market, as an undesirable place to be. Whether their rate of exit has been faster or slower than that of the general population, is perhaps worthy of investigation, but has not been investigated here.

APPENDIX E

"Other Comments" to a Questionnaire Conducted in Auckland, N.Z.*

1. In general, I would say, tenants always promise to be co-operative, do the garden, always so grateful when we assign them a flat (at a very modest rental), but in a very short time they let everything look untidy. I find it a big hassle reletting a flat. We have had the flats legally divided on cross leases and could sell easily, but right now we are undecided. Each flat is moderately valued at $50,000 and the average weekly rent is $66 so by the time we pay rates, etc., and maintenance, we'd really be well rid of them.

2. Having worked very hard as a builder and having saved my money and been chief Dogs Body, mown lawns, cleaned stove, moved rubbish, all these things I accepted as part of the job, but to have controls come in June 1982, controlling my money and property, I find unfair. If the government wants to control housing why not buy all my property off me and use it for State housing? I am still paying 17-18 percent mortgage money and on the rents received am now in a loss situation and cannot get 11 percent money (not available).

    My Bank now tells me that I can no longer have overdraft facility secured on property but have to arrange a term personal loan (higher interest).

3. Did have three flats and one house for rent prior to ten-year tax law.

    Sold three flats because did not want to get forced into holding for such a long time.

    Rental domestic properties economically more attractive before rent freeze and ten-year law.

4. Not a typical situation as rental is significantly lower than market levels to ensure satisfactory long term tenancy by reasonable tenants usually young marrieds saving for own home. Satisfactory for 15 years for both parties but certainly not an economic proposition.

5. Because of increased pressure on landlords there are becoming less rental units available which means that people will become increasingly dependent on the tax payer for accommodation. This is a bad trend.

    Tax deductible interest for young families as in the USA may alleviate some of those problems.

*This is reprinted from "New Zealand National Housing Commission Research Report," Lehrer, 1984, appendix 3, pp. 168-74.

6. I am now more or less retired and in the past eight years or so have lived in what would be known as a home and income property where *very* careful selection of tenants has guaranteed careful occupation and congenial relationships. That the rents are substantially below a fair market rate makes no change to the tenants' attitude towards the units they occupy and I find that I have to employ gardening services when away from the units.

    Prior to retirement I was responsible for the management of several hundred flats and houses in the Auckland area and grew increasingly concerned with the plethora of legislation aimed at regulating tenancy matters but which served only as a hindrance to good landlords who actually are in the greater majority and as a wonderful tool in the hands of many tenants, solicitors and government employees for the complete frustration and loss to good landlords.

    The almost impossible hope of obtaining redress through the over-loaded legal system has to be experienced to be believed and just one bad tenant aided and abetted by a smart solicitor or other adviser can quite literally create mayhem amongst other tenants in the block and create a substantial financial loss to the owner. Most regrettably his only real recourse to protect his income and property is on the verge of being illegal and is certainly fraught with risk of legal or physical reprisal.

    The situation has now arisen where rental housing stock in the private sector has received no new blood for some years. The true situation has been masked first by the emigration of many of our young trades-people and secondly by the grouping up of many low income families who are jobless and unable to meet the cost of rent. There will be a number of other masking factors also.

    When our little country experiences an end to the present recession and our standard of living commences to rise there will be a shortage of rental accommodation on a scale not experienced before. If government does no more than it is doing at present and that is trying to regulate the situation then I am frightened of the consequences.

    Were the private landlord given more control of his property and were government to offer incentives to build then the private sector would rise to the occasion. There must be a reasonable return possible and better recognition of an owner's rights. Surely this can be done without releasing him from the need for fair dealing and at the same time controlling the greedy and thoughtless owner.

7. Most tenants take umbrage when you deduct $10 to $20 from their bond for leaving the stove and flat generally dirty, when it has always been my practice to ensure the flat is spotless when they move in. The rent freeze has been unfair to most landlords, particularly the allowable increases, when a property is well below market value now the wage freeze has been lifted.

8. The greatest drawback is constant hounding from Inland Revenue Department—generally wanting to know how you have been able to gain valuable property on the income one is earning and wanting to know how you can possibly service huge mortgage.

    In ten years I've sold my family home—original cost $28,000 and then bought another badly run down place, done it up, working 100 hours a week, sold it, bought another house in bad state of repair and repeated this process several times. Now after 10 years of solid slog, not being able to join social clubs (because of changing districts), living in old clothes and making my children all work spare time on renovations and partially depriving them of full sport and social activities we finally made it to the "house of our dreams" which we again worked hard at renovating [on] two incomes. Flats are necessary to offset huge rates (prestigious area) and big insurance. I've only been a wage earner right through. Have paid PAYE tax and had no other income. Yet Inland Revenue has hassled me constantly, seeking to know how I got to be in a valuable property from humble beginnings and obviously not able to get there on wages.

    Ten years of my life devoted to attaining a high standard of living—through sheer determination, self sacrifice and hard work only to be subjected to the third degree.

    That's why we are leaving N.Z. forever.

9. I do have very good tenants but have attractive units and am very fussy in picking tenants but I do feel that 2 weeks' bond is by long not enough. Tenants hardly have to do anything in damage and bond money is not enough. I personally have had no problems at all with tenants but talking to other landlords, tenants can do a lot of wear and tear and 2 weeks' bond is not getting you anywhere.

10. Like any form of investment, when it becomes uneconomical and there are too many problems in the running of it, you change your investment to something more lucrative, and when all is said and done it is only one form of investment.

    And I don't think any landlord is in the rental property business for any other reason.

11. I and my family are a "small investor." Total net assets of the family are under $100,000. This property investment was commenced in approximately 1973-74 with a view to:

    (a)invest time and effort;

    (b)accept some financial risk; and

    (c)gain some capital reward (cash rewards expected to be approximately nil on average).

    This in my view was a reasonable business investment. However retroactive alteration of the "rules" has destroyed this opportunity. The result is that the net return from capital *and* cash is now around $20 per hour. I have other business avenues which can yield *more* than $20 per hour with less financial strain and less rental management "hassle." On the presumption that the government wanted to make rental property ownership less attractive they have certainly achieved this. The block of five units that I am selling is going, I am told, to be split up and sold to home owners.

My personal opinion of the recent legislation is that it is oppressive, draconian in retrospective action and totally abhorrent to a free society. I have been in my view a "good" landlord charging fair rents for good properties. The tenants were happy and so was I. Why did the government change things!!

12. Problems: cats, dogs, cars on lawns, careless parking, undue noise, radios, untidiness, uncleanliness, inconsiderateness. Many tenants have no cleaning detergents, vacuum cleaners or incentive to keep clean their units (especially under 25). Most tenants under 25 use the unit as a serviced hotel room or motel and have no desire to keep the place up to scratch.

13. This was my way of investing inherited money. I want to help my three sons get their own homes in the future.

Should I lose my job or retire, it is a security—I'll have some income.

14. Our flats are very modern and up-to-date in "as new" condition in a very good position (in Gladstone Road, Parnell) rented for $80 to $85 which is very reasonable for the area.

Unfortunately I have found to my dismay dealing with the type of people who rent flats is not at all easy and have been sadly disillusioned over the past four years. It is no joke to have a new tenant say on oath that he is going to be permanent and then with little or no notice leave after a month leaving a very dirty flat for the owner to clean up. Perhaps if the government intends to change the law to give the tenant more security of tenure it could also be made to work the other way as well to give the landlord the same rights!!

15. Have already recently obtained vacant possession of two flats and am doing them up for sale. I am not prepared to subsidize tenants and have my rents restricted when commercial properties are not so restricted.

16. Rents are virtually frozen. My return was approximately 6 percent of market value. Then I pay 66 percent personal tax out of this. Leaves 2 percent which is ludicrous. I am getting out.

17. In general the great unfavourable aspect of tenanted properties is that tenants observe no responsibility in caring for the property—the attitude is "leave it to the landlord"! The real estate rent collecting agents, in our experience do nothing to supervise the properties and personal checking is constantly required by the owners.

All of the flats are modern except four in a large house subdivided under an architect with completely separate facilities. All are maintained by the owners—repairs and redecoration performed immediately as required. In one or two exceptions tenants have redecorated themselves but this is not encouraged because of lack of tradesman quality in the work.

It is true that many of our investment properties have shown good profits. This is because the units erected in 1965 cost (finished) approximately $6,000 each. No doubt a replacement at today's cost would be $36,000 each. On the other hand two other single units at $28,000 and $65,000, respectively at Mission Bay and Kohimarama in most select areas 50 yards from waterfront, purchased in 1978 and 1982, are not favourable on aspect of return on investment in respect of rents. Of course, the probable capital appreciation must be taken into account as an important plus factor.

But it is clear that investment at today's prices for new units is simply not economic on rent return. The general run of tenants cannot afford or will not pay rents much in excess of $80 a week even in select areas. Thus inflation has created a remarkable anomaly and a solution to the problem is not very evident.

Bearing in mind that a two bedroom modern unit in Auckland cannot be purchased for under $40,000; interest on $40,000 at 11% p.a. is in excess of $80 per week to which must be added rates, insurance and upkeep—probably $20 a week. Thus a $40,000 unit should not let at under $100 per week. Obviously a tenant renting such a unit at under $100 a week is well-placed and probably wise to stay put.

The flat was my deceased mother's. For first few years I was soft and let it to friends or friends of friends at a low rental, and collected rents myself. In general tenants did not look after or appreciate low rental (one redecorated—I supplied material). Two years ago, after a very bad experience I put it in the hands of Barfoot & Thompson who immediately let it at a considerably higher rental. I am not fit to be a landlord, as I am too soft. I need a professional manager to look after things, which I now have.

18. Tenants find it difficult sometimes to raise the bond money as well as agent's fees and rent in advance. By establishing an insurance to guarantee amount of bond to landlord, an adequate sum could be provided to cover wilful or excessive damage by tenants, who would be able to pay the relative premium in installments. (The underwriters or Housing Corporation would thereby have a record of any re-offending tenants who claimed regularly on their insurance.)

19. The "small" landlord has been thwarted by government rent decrees. We provide a service and are almost benevolent, but if we can't show a fair return on the total capital value, we would be foolish to continue.

My last rental loss was refused by Inland Revenue Department, which has put a negative angle on the situation.

20. Investing in rental accommodation is not worthwhile any more:
   (a) too much hassle (insurance, rates, maintenance, etc.);

(b) too low net-return and hardly any capital gain against inflation;

(c) money not readily available if needed.

21. With present rental regulations preventing a rent increase of more than 3 percent property rented at $45 per week since 1979 is not returning minimum interest—it would be better sold and money invested.

22. My biggest fear and hate with rental properties is how I am allowed to get tenants, and that my rights when they have to be evicted are stacked against me. To me it seems it does not pay to have good rental places, you stand to lose too much if you get a bad tenant.

23. I have managed flats for a long time, I advertize and let my own flats choosing my tenants. For the last few years we have put rents up. Before the rent freeze I find I get a much better type of tenant, my son and I both work in maintaining the property's lawns, painting, papering, maintaining washing machines, etc. We are called on quite a lot. They (the tenants) just sign a rent book with seven days either way for notice to quit. If for some reason they leave without notice I forget about that. This has not happened a lot but we do get the odd one. An empty flat is better than a bad tenant.

I would not advise anyone to go in for flats unless they have the time to put into them and know their own tenants and being able to do your own work—cleaning, papering and painting and keeping the drains clear.

The city council is rather hard charging $172.50 for water whether you use that much or not and then the rates go up each year, I am paying the most on the road.

24. I was a landlord of four superior flats from 1975 to 1983 and I sold them in 1983 for the following reasons:

(a) The rent freeze caught me with my best flats cheaper than the others;

(b) Interest rates on mortgages rose from 16 to 20 percent while rents were frozen;

(c) Rents were 60 to 80 percent of their market value. Hence I was subsidizing my tenant's living expenses who were generally well-to-do executives;

(d) I sold to a developer who converted them to individual apartments which he sold well;

(e) I would never own rental accommodation again because of *gross government interference with the business.*

BIBLIOGRAPHY

Abella I. and Troper H. *None is Too Many*. Toronto: Lester and Orpen Dennis, 1982.

Achtenberg, E. *A Tenant's Guide to Rent Control in Massachusetts*. Cambridge: Urban Planning Aid, Inc., 1973(A).

_____. *Less Rent, More Control*. Cambridge: Urban Planning Aid, Inc., 1973(B).

_____. "The Social Utility of Rent Control." In *Housing Urban America*, edited by J. Pynos and C. Hartman. Chicago: Aldine Pub., 1973(C).

Allaun, F. *No Place Like Home—Britain's Housing Tragedy*. London: Andre Deutsch, 1972.

Arendt, H. Eichman in Jerusalem. New York: Viking Press, 1965.

Arnott, R. Rent Control and Options for Decontrol in Ontario. Toronto: Ontario Economic Council, 1981.

Aron, R. "Social Class, Ruling Class, Political Class." In *Power in Societies*, edited by M. Olsen. New York: Macmillan, 1970.

Beirne, P. *Fair Rent and Legal Fiction—Housing Legislation in a Capitalist Society*. London: Macmillan, 1977.

Bell, D. *The Coming of Post-Industrial Society*. New York: Basic Books, 1973.

_____. *The Cultural Contradictions of Capitalism*. New York: Basic Books, 1976.

Bentham, J. *Security and Equality of Property*. London: Bowring, 1843; reprinted in *Property*, edited by C.B. Macpherson. Toronto: University of Toronto Press, 1978.

Beresford, J.C. and A.M. Rivlin. "Privacy, Poverty and Old Age." *Demography* 3 (1966): 247-58.

Berger, P. *The Sacred Canopy*. New York: Doubleday, 1967.

Berger, P. and T. Luckman. *The Social Construction of Reality*. New York: Doubleday, 1966.

Bierstedt, R. "An Analysis of Social Power." *American Sociological Review*, vol. 15 (December 1950): 730-38.

Birkenfield v. City of Berkeley, Case No. 428971, California Superior Court, 1972; Court of Appeals 1 Civil 34378, 1975.

Blau, P.M. and Duncan Blau. "Measuring the Status of Occupations" 1967a. In *Social Mobility*, edited by Coxon and Jones. Middlesex: Penguin, 1975.

_____. "The Process of Stratification" 1967b. In *Social Mobility*, edited by Coxon and Jones. Middlesex: Penguin, 1975.

Blau, P.M. and M.W. Meyer. *Bureaucracy in Modern Society*. New York: Random House, 1956.

Block, W. *Defending the Undefendable*. New York: Fleet Press, 1976.

Block, W. and E. Olsen. *Rent Control—Myths and Realities*. Vancouver: Fraser Institute, 1981.

Bloomberg, L.N. "Rent Control and the Housing Shortage: A Commentary on 'Roofs or Ceilings?' by Friedman and Stigler." *Journal of Land and Public Utility Economics*, 23 (1947): 214-18.

Bordessa, R. "The Real Estate Agent as English Country Gentleman." *Real Estate Review*, N.P. 1979.

Bott, E. *Family and Social Network: Roles, norms, and external relationships*. London: Tavistock, 1964.

Bottomore, T. "Elites and Society" (1964). In *Power in Societies*, edited by M. Olsen. New York: Macmillan, 1970.

Bracknell, C. "Picking the Right Landlord," *Singles*, 27 (August 1979).

Braverman, H. *Labour and Monopoly Capital*. N.Y. Monthly Review Press, 1974.

Brennan, J. and J. Rawlings. "Laws That Make Slum Landlords," "The Twilight World of New Rachmanism and Poverty," and "Decline of the Private Landlord." *Financial Weekly* (18 February 1980): 1, 4, and 5.

Brenner, J.F. and H.M. Franklin. *Rent Control in North America and Four European Countries*. Washington, D.C.: Potomac Institute, 1977.

Bucknall, B. "Rent Review in Ontario." *Housing and People*, 8, no. 2 (Fall-Winter 1977): 8-15.

Bureau of Municipal Research. *Be It Ever So Humble*. Toronto: Civic Affairs, 1977.

Burney, E. *Housing on Trial—A Study of Immigrants and Local Government*. London: Oxford University Press, 1967.

Canadian Council on Social Development. *A Review of Canadian Social Housing Policy*. Toronto: CCSD, 1977.

Carr, E. *The House of All Sorts*. Toronto: Clarke, Irwin, 1944.

Carr, E.H. *What is History?* Middlesex: Penguin, 1964.

Central Mortgage and Housing Corporation, Program and Market Requirements Division. *Impact of Rent Controls Under Varying Market Conditions*. Ottawa: CMHC, 1978.

Chapman, R. "To Rent or Buy." Ph.D. diss., University of Auckland, N.Z., 1981.

Cheung, S.N.S. "Roofs or Stars: The stated intents and actual effects of a rental ordinance." *Economic Enquiry*, 13: 1-21.

Clement, W. *The Canadian Corporate Elite*. Toronto: McClelland & Stewart, 1975.

Cohen D. "The Agony of Interest Rates." *Canadian Business*, June 1980.

Community Research and Publications Group. *Less Rent More Control: A Tenant's Guide to Rent Control in Massachusetts*. Cambridge, Mass.: Urban Planning Aid, Inc., 1973.

Coser, L. *The Functions of Social Conflict*. New York: Free Press, Macmillan, 1956.

Cragg, J.G. *Rent Control Report*. Victoria: Legislature of British Columbia, 1974.

Craig, J. and K. Lehrer. "An Inventory of Propositions Towards a Theory of Co-Operative Communities." *Journal of Rural Co-Operation*, 7, no. 1-2, 1979.

Cross, M. *Local Government and Politics*. London: Longman, 1978.

Cullingworth, J.B. *Essays on Housing Policy: The British Scene*. London: George Allen & Unwin, 1979.

———. *Housing in Transition: A Case Study in the City of Lancaster, 1958-1962*. London: Heinemann, 1963.

Cutting, M. *Housing Rights Handbook*. London: Shelter, 1974.

Dahlie, J. and T. Fernando, eds. "Reflections on Ethnicity and the Exercise of Power: An Introductory Note." *Ethnicity, Power & Politics in Canada*. Toronto: Methuen, 1981.

Dahrendorf, R. "Social Structure, Group Interest, and Conflict Groups." In *Power in Societies*, edited by M. Olson. New York: Macmillan, 1970.

Dalstrom, E. *Efficiency, Satisfaction and Democracy at Work.* Mimeo. University of Gottenberg, 1977.

De Toqueville, A. *Democracy in America.* New York: Vintage Books, 1945.

Diamond, S. "The Rule of Law Versus the Order of Custom"

Donnison, D.V. *The Government of Housing.* Harmondsworth: Penguin, 1967, p. 85.

Durkheim, E. *The Division of Labour in Society.* New York: Free Press, 1947.

Eckstein, E. "A Theory of Stable Democracy." Appendix B. of *Division and Cohesion in Democracy.* Princeton University Press, 1966.

Eldridge, J.E.T. "Max Weber—some comments, problems and continuities." Introductory Essay to *The Interpretation of Social Reality.* New York: Charles Scribner's Sons, 1971.

Emerson, R. "Power-Dependence Relations." In *Power in Societies*, edited by M. Olsen. London: Collier-Macmillan, 1970.

Emery, F.E. and E.L. Trist. "The Causal Texture of Organizational Environments." *Human Relations* 18 (1965): 21-31.

Engels, F. *The Housing Question.* Progress Publishers, 1970.

Etzioni, A. *A Comparative Analysis of Complex Organizations.* New York: Free Press, 1961.

_____. *The Semi-Professions and Their Organization.* New York: Free Press, 1969.

_____. "Power as a Societal Force." In *Power in Societies*, edited by M. Olsen. New York: Macmillan, 1970.

Evans-Pritchard, E.E. *Witchcraft, Oracles and Magic Among the Azande.* Oxford: Clarendon Press, 1958.

Eversley, D. "Landlords' Slow Goodbye." *New Society*, January 16, 1975.

Fallis, G. *Housing Programs and Income Distribution in Ontario.* Toronto: O.E.C./University of Toronto Press, 1980.

Fanon, F. *The Wretched of the Earth.* New York: Grove Press, 1967.

Fiedler, F.A. *Theory of Leadership Effectiveness.* New York: McGraw-Hill, 1967.

Fish, S. and M. Dennis. *Programs in Search of a Policy: Low Income Housing in Canada.* Toronto: Hakkert, 1972.

Forster, E.M. *Howard's End*. Harmondsworth, England: Penguin, 1941.

Fox, A. *Beyond Contract*. London: Faber & Faber, 1974.

French, J.R.P. and B. Raven. "The Bases of Social Power." In *Group Dynamics*. 2d ed., edited by Cartwright and Zander. Evanston, Illinois: Row, Peterson, 1960.

French, J.R.P., J. Israel and D. Aas. "An Experiment in Participation in a Norwegian Factory." *Human Relations* 13, no. 1 (1960): 3-19.

Friedman, M. and G.J. Stigler. "Roofs or Ceilings?—The Current Housing Problem." *Popular Essays on Current Problems* I, no. 2 (September 1946).

Galbraith, J.K. *The New Industrial State*. Boston: Houghton Mifflin, 1967.

_____. "The Theory of Countervailing Power." In *Power in Society*, edited by M. Olsen. New York: Macmillan, 1970.

Gauldie, E. *Cruel Habitations*. London: George Allen & Unwin, 1974.

Gerth, H.H. and C.W. Mills, eds. *From Max Weber: Essays in Sociology*. New York: Oxford University Press, 1946.

Goffman, E. *The Presentation of Self in Everyday Life*. Garden City, New York: Doubleday, 1959.

_____. *Asylums*. New York: Doubleday, 1961.

Goldenberg, S. *Men of Property*. Personal Library, Everest House, 1982.

Government of the Republic of China. *La Cour Des Faumages*. Peking, 1968.

Graham, A., et al. *Rent Controls—Why We Need Them*. Social Planning Council of Metropolitan Toronto, 1975.

Grebler, L. *Housing Market Behaviour in a Declining Area*. New York: Glumbia V.P., 1952.

_____. "Implications of Rent Control Experience in the United States." *International Labour Review* 65 (1952): 470.

Habermas, J. *Legitimation Crisis*. London: Heinemann Educational Books, 1976.

Habitat. *National Report for the United Nations Conference on Human Settlement*. Bonn, 1967: 37.

Harloe, M., R. Issacharoff and R. Minns. "The Organizational Context of Housing Policy in Inner London: The Lambeth Experience." Paper presented at The Inner City, a conference on research and policy for London, 1972.

Hartman, C. "The Big Squeeze." *Politics Today*, May-June 1978.

Harvey, D. *Social Justice and the City*. Maryland: Johns Hopkins University Press, 1973.

Hayek, F.A., et al. *Verdict on Rent Control*. Reading no. 7. London: Institute of Economic Affairs, 1972.

Hayek, F.A., et al. *Rent Control—A Popular Paradox*. Vancouver: Fraser Institute, 1975.

Hayek, F.A., *Rent Control: Myths and Realities*. Vancouver: Fraser Institute, 1981.

Heung, R. *The Do's and Don'ts of Housing Policy: The Case of British Columbia*. Vancouver: Fraser Institute, 1976.

Homans, G. *The Human Group*. New York: Harcourt Brace Jovanovich Inc., 1950.

Horngren, C. *Cost Accounting: A Managerial Emphasis*. Englewood Cliffs, N.J.: Prentice-Hall, 1982.

Howe, I. *World of Our Fathers*. New York: Harcourt Brace Jovanovich, 1976.

Hughes, E. *The Sociological Eye*. Chicago: Aldine Atherton, 1971.

Interdepartmental Study Team. *Housing and Rent Controls in British Columbia*, Government of B.C., 1975.

Jamieson, S.M. *Times of Trouble: Labour Unrest and Industrial Conflict in Canada, 1900-1966*. Study no. 22, Ministry of Supply and Services, Canada, 1976.

Kafka, F. *Short Stories*. Edited by J.M.S. Pasley. London: Oxford University Press, 1963.

_____. "Before the Law." In *The Complete Stories*, edited by N.N. Glatzer. New York: Schocken, 1946.

_____. *The Castle*. New York: Knopf, 1954.

Kilmartin, L. and D.C. Thomas. *Cities Unlimited: The Sociology of Urban Development in Australia and New Zealand*. Sydney: Allen & Unwin, 1978.

Housing and Development Administration of New York City v. Community Housing Improvement Program, Inc.

Koestler, A. *The Gladiators*. New York: Macmillan, 1947.

Krohn, R.G., B. Fleming, and M. Manzer. *The Other Economy—The Internal Logic of Local Rental Housing*. Canadian Experience Series, Peter Martin Associates, 1979.

Kropotkin, P. *Mutual Aid*. New York: McClure Phillips & Co., 1902.

Lappin, B.W. and M. Ross. *Community Organization: Theory, Principles and Practice*. New York: Harper, 1967.

Laverty P. *The Impact of Rent Review on Rental Housing in Ontario*. Ministry of Municipal Affairs and Housing Research Staff Report. Toronto: Province of Ontario, 1982.

Lawrence, P. and J. Lorsch. *Organization and Environment*. Cambridge, Mass.: Harvard University Press, 1967.

Lehrer, K. "Social and Administrative Issues in Condominium and Rental Housing." Mimeo. Toronto: York University, 1976.

_____. "Industrial Democracy—A Comparative Analysis." M.A. Research—Review paper. Toronto: York University, 1978.

_____. and J.G. Craig. "An Inventory of Propositions Towards a Theory of Co-Operative Communities." *Journal of Rural Co-Operation* 7, no. 1-2, 1979.

_____. "Power, Organization, Professionalization and the State—A Search for Linkages." Mimeo. Toronto: York University, 1980. (A)

_____. "Professionalization and the Evolution of Power." Paper presented at Ontario Association of Sociologists and Anthropologists, Annual Conference, Guelph, 1980. (B)

_____. "Some Expected Effects of the World Oil Situation on Property Markets, with Particular Reference to Southern Ontario." *Canadian Real Estate Journal*, Spring 1980. (C)

_____. "Conversion of Rental Properties to Condominium or Co-Operative Complexes—Rationale and Problems." Canadian Real Estate Journal, Summer 1980.

_____. "Housing, Rent and Regulation." Working paper presented at conference on urban political economy, American University, Washington, 1981. (A)

_____. "Power Base Options for the Individual Worker—Professionalization, Unionization and Worker Control." Mimeo. Toronto: York University, 1981. (B)

_____. "Rent Controls—The Causes and Effects of Interventionist Policies." Toronto: Centre for Real Estate Expertise, York University, 1981.

_____. "Power, Participation and the Regulation of Rent." Mimeo. Toronto: York University, 1984. (A)

_____. "A Profile of the Private Residential Landlord in Auckland, and his Role in Rental Housing." Research study commissioned by New Zealand National Housing Commission, 1984. (B)

Lett, M. *Rent Control: Concepts, Realities and Mechanisms.* New Jersey: Center for Urban Policy Research, Rutger State University, 1976.

Lewis, O. *The Children of Sanchez.* New York: Random House, 1961.

_____. *La Vida.* New York: Random House, 1966.

Linton, R., ed. *The Science of Man in the World Crisis.* New York: Columbia University Press, 1945.

Lipset, S.M. "Social Conflict, Legitimacy and Democracy." In *Power in Societies*, edited by M. Olsen. New York: Macmillan, 1970.

Lipsky, M. *Rent Strikes: Poor Man's Weapon.* Madison Institute for Research on Poverty, University of Wisconsin, 1909.

Lubbock, R. "Vile Bodies We Should Love," *Quest* 6, issue 7, December 1977.

Macchiavelli, N. *The Prince.* New York: Mentor, 1952.

Macpherson, C.B. *The Life and Times of Liberal Democracy.* New York: Oxford University Press, 1977.

_____. *Possessive Individualism.* New York: Oxford University Press, 1977.

_____. *Property.* New York: Oxford University Press, 1978.

Marcuse, P. *Rental Housing in the City of New York.* New York: Department of Housing Preservation and Development, 1979.

Marx, K. and Engels, F. "The Manifesto of the Communist Party." In *Power in Societies*, edited by M. Olsen. New York: Macmillan, 1970.

_____. *Capital.* London: Everyman, 1972.

_____. *Early Writings.* Translated and edited by T. Bottomore. New York: McGraw-Hill, 1964.

Maxwell, M. and J. Maxwell *Professional Aspirations and Social Structure: The Case of Occupational Therapy.* Paper presented at the Canadian Learned Societies CSAA Annual Conference, Saskatoon, 1979.

Mayhew, L. "Stability and Change in Legal Systems." In *Stability and Social Change*, edited by B. Barber and A. Inkeles. Boston: Little Brown & Co., 1971.

McAfee, A. et al. *Housing Families at High Densities*. Planning Department, City of Vancouver, 1978.

McCormack, R. "Cloth Caps and Jobs: The Ethnicity of English Immigrants in Canada." In *Ethnicity, Power & Politics in Canada*, edited by J. Dahlie and T. Fernando. Toronto: Methuen, 1981.

McInnes, R. *Landlord/Tenant Rights in Ontario*. Vancouver: Self-Counsel Press, 1980.

McLuhan, M. and Q. Fiore. *The Medium is the Massage*. New York: Random House, 1967.

Merton, R.K. *Social Theory and Social Structure*. Glencoe, Ill.: Free Press, 1963.

Michels, R. "The Iron Law of Oligarchy." In *Power in Societies*, edited by M. Olsen. New York: Macmillan, 1970.

_____. *Political Parties: A Sociological Study of the Oligarchical Tendencies of Modern Democracy*. New York: Free Press, 1949.

Mills, C.W. "The Power Elite" (1965). In *Power in Societies*, edited by M. Olsen. New York: Macmillan, 1970.

_____. *White Collar*. New York: Oxford University Press, 1956.

Milner Holland Committee. *Report of the Committee on Housing in Greater London*. London: HMSO, 1965.

Miron, J.R. and J.B. Cullingworth. *Rent Control: Impacts on Income Distribution, Affordability, and Security of Tenure*. Toronto: Centre for Urban and Community Studies, University of Toronto, 1983.

Moorhouse, J.C. "Optimal Housing Maintenance Under Rent Control." *Southern Economic Journal* 39 (July 1972): 100.

Mortgage Insurance Co. of Canada. "Survey of Real Estate and Mortgage Markets." *Globe & Mail, Report on Business*, 7 April 1980.

Mosca, G. "The Ruling Class." In *Power in Societies, edited by M. Olsen. New York: Macmillan, 1970.*

Mosier, M.M. and R.A. Soble. "Modern Legislation, Metropolitan Court, Minuscule Results: A Study of Detroit's Landlord-tenant Court." *University of Michigan's Journal of Law Reform* 9, (1973) 9-70.

Neumann, J.V. and D. Morgenstern. *Theory of Games and Economic Behaviour*. Princeton: Princeton University Press, 1947.

Nevitt, A.A. "The Nature of Rent Controlling Legislation in the U.K." London: Centre for Environmental Studies, University Working Paper 8, 1970.

Olsen, E.O. *The Effects of a Simple Rent Control Scheme on a Competitive Housing Market*. Santa Monica, California: Rand Corporation, 1969.

Ontario Provincial Ministry of Municipal Affairs and Housing Research Staff. *The Impact of Rent Review on Rental Housing in Ontario* (The "Laverty Study"). Province of Ontario, 1982.

Ontario Legislative Assembly. *Report of the Standing General Committee on Policy* Paper 13 (Green paper). Toronto: Ministry of Government Services, 1978.

Orwell, G. *Keep the Aspidistra Flying*. U.K.: Penguin, 1962.

_____. *Down and Out in Paris and London*. London: Secker and Warburg, 1949.

Parsons, T. "Social Classes and Class Conflict." *American Economic Review* XXXIX (1949): 16-26.

_____. "The Monopoly of Force and the 'Power Bank'." In *Power in Societies*, edited by M. Olsen. New York: Macmillan, 1970.

_____. *Social Systems and the Evolution of Action Theory*. New York: Free Press, 1977.

Pateman, C. *Participation and Democratic Theory*. Cambridge: Cambridge University Press, 1970.

Patterson, J. and K. Watson. *Rent Stabilization—A Review of Current Policies in Canada*. Canadian Council on Social Development, 1976.

Perrow, C. *Complex Organizations: A Critical Essay*. 2d ed. Illinois: Scott, Foresman & Co., 1979.

Porter, J. *The Vertical Mosaic*. Toronto: University of Toronto Press, 1965.

Presthus, R. *The Organizational Society*. New York: St. Martin's Press, 1978.

Rawls, J. *A Theory of Justice*. Cambridge: M.I.T. Press, 1971.

Rex, J. *Race-Relations in Sociological Theory*. New York: Schorken Books, 1970.

Rex, J. and R. Moore. *Race, Community and Conflict—A Study of Sparkbrook*. London: Oxford University Press, 1967.

Richmond, A.H. "Migration, Housing and Urban Planning in Toronto." In *Current Research in Sociology*. The Hague: Mouton & Co., 1974.

Rodegard, L.R. *Power and Spatial Justice*. Mimeo. Toronto: York University, 1982.

Rose, A. *Canadian Housing Policies, 1935-1980*. Toronto: Butterworth, 1980.

Rose, J.G. *Landlords and Tenants*. New Brunswick, N.J.: Transaction Books, 1973.

Ross, E.A. *The Principles of Sociology*. New York: The Century Co., 1920.

Ross, M. *Case Histories in Community Organization*. New York: Harper, 1958.

Rousseau, J.J. *The Social Contract*. London: Dent, 1935.

_____. *Emile*. 1911.

Russell, J.R. *Cases in Urban Management*. Cambridge: M.I.T. Press, 1974.

Rydenfelt, S. "Swedish Housing Policy, 1942-1972: History and Analysis." *Skandinaviska Enskilda Banken Quarterly Review*, Stockholm, 1972.

Sartori, G. *Democratic Theory*. Detroit: Wayne State University Press, 1962.

Saunders, P. *Urban Politics—A Sociological Interpretation*. Middlesex: Penguin Education, 1980.

Schiff, M. and A.Y. Lewin. *Behavioural Aspects of Accounting*. Englewood Cliffs, N.J.: Prentice-Hall, 1974.

Schumpeter, J. *Capitalism, Socialism and Democracy*. London: Allen & Unwin, 1943.

Shils, E.A. "Socialism in America." *University Observer* I: 1947.

Simmel, G. *Conflict and The Web of Group Affiliations*. Translated by K. Wolff and R. Bendix. New York: Free Press, Macmillan, 1955.

Simon, H.A. *Administrative Behaviour*. New York: Free Press, 1947.

_____. "On the Concept of Organizational Goals." *ASQ* 9, (June 1964): 1-22.

_____. "Notes on the Observation and Measurement of Political Power." In *The Search for Community Power*, edited by W.D. Hawley and F.M. Wirt, 1968.

Smith, L.B. *Anatomy of a Crisis—Canadian Housing Policy in the Seventies*. Vancouver: Fraser Institute, 1977.

Smith, L.B. and P. Tomlinson. "Rent Controls in Ontario: Roofs or Ceilings?" *Journal of the American Real Estate and Urban Economics Association*, Summer 1981.

Social Planning Council of Metropolitan Toronto. *Rent Controls: Why we need them. What kind? How long?* Toronto, 1975.

Social Planning Council of Metropolitan Toronto. *The Rent Race*. Toronto, 1974.

Society of Labour Lawyers. *The End of the Private Landlord*. London: Fabian Society, 1973.

Sorokin, P. *Social and Cultural Mobility*. New York: Free Press, 1959.

Standing Committee on Administration of Justice, Province of Ontario. *Report on the Ontario Housing Corporation and Local Housing Authorities*, Queens Park, 1981.

Sternlieb, G. *The Urban Housing Dilemma*. New York: New York City Housing and Development Administration, 1972.

Sternlieb, G. and R.W. Burchell. *Residential Abandonment—The Tenement Landlord Revisited*. New Jersey: Center for Urban Policy Research, Rutgers University, 1973.

Sternlieb, G. and J.W. Hughes. *Housing and Economic Reality*. New Jersey: Center for Urban Policy Research, Rutgers University, 1976.

Sternlieb, G. *The Tenement Landlord*. New Jersey: Rutgers University, 1966.

Sunahara, A.G. "Deportation: The Final Solution to Canada's 'Japanese Problem.'" In *Ethnicity, Power & Politics in Canada*, edited by J. Dahlie and T. Fernando. Toronto: Methuen, 1981.

Terreberry, S. "The Evolution of Organizational Environments." Ph.D. course paper, University of Michigan Mimeo, 1967, pp. 1-37.

Thernstrom, S. *The Other Bostonians—Poverty and Progress in the American Metropolis, 1880-1970*. Cambridge: Harvard University Press, 1972.

Von Mises, L. *Human Action: A Treatise on Economics*. New Haven: Yale University Press, 1949.

Wagley, C. and M. Harris. *Minorities in the New World*. New York: Columbia University Press, 1964.

Walker, M. "What Are the Concepts?" *Rent Control—A Popular Paradox*. Vancouver: The Fraser Institute, 1975.

Weber, M. "Bureaucracy and Law." In *From Max Weber—Essays in Sociology*, translated by H.H. Gerth and C.W. Mills. New York: Oxford University Press, 1946.

_____. *The Theory of Social and Economic Organization*. Translated by Henderson and Talcott Parsons. New York: Oxford University Press, 1947.

_____. *The Protestant Ethic and the Spirit of Capitalism*. Translated by T. Parsons. New York: Scribner, 1958.

_____. *The Interpretation of Social Reality*. New York: Charles Scribner's Sons, 1971.

Wexler, H.J. and R. Peak. *Housing and Local Government—A Research Guide for Policy Makers and Planners*. Massachusetts: Lexington Books, 1975.

Wheeler, M. *The Right to Housing*. Montreal: Harvest House, 1969.

Wickberg, E. "Chinese Organizations and the Canadian Political Process: Two Case Studies." In *Ethnicity, Power & Politics in Canada*, edited by J. Dahlie and T. Fernando. Toronto: Methuen, 1981.

Willis, J.W. "A Short History of Rent Control Laws." *Cornell Law Quarterly* 36 (1950): 84.

Wilson, R. "Metro Reaches Age of Maturity on Threshold of New Era." *Metropolitan Toronto Business Journal*, Fall 1979.

Wolin, S. *Politics and Vision*. Boston: Little, Brown and Co., 1960.

Wood, J. "A Visible Minority Votes." In *Ethnicity, Power & Politics in Canada*, edited by J. Dahlie and T. Fernando. Toronto: Methuen, 1981.

Zola, E. *Germinal*. New York: New American Library, 1970.

Bibliography: Newspaper Articles

The Economist, "Aggro is always in season," 23 December 1980.

Globe and Mail, "Anxious house buyers resigned to massive mortgages: The victims of high interest," 25 May 1981, 1.

_____, "Tenant group supports revision of rent review," 17 November 1982, 5.

_____, "Once mighty Tanenbaum empire fights for life," 19 March 1983, B1.

_____, "Hill says text on race not enough for police," 17 July 1983.

London Financial Times, "Squatters' protests highlight serious problem," Netherlands Supplement, 23 December 1980, 7.*Now*, "Tenants feisty in '82," 23 December 1982-5 January 1983, 5.

Shelterforce, "The Tenant Vote: How Groups Use Elections to Win Political Power," 6 , no. 2 (May 1981): 6-7.

Toronto Star, "Unhealthy Cut in Rent Controls," Editorial, 27 March 1980, A6.

_____, "Greedy owners, vicious tenants, everyone's losing in Parkdale," 26 April 1980, A14.

_____, "Homeowners: Don't look to government for mortgage help—Trudeau," 16 May 1981, A1.

_____, "No More Aid to Consumers Trudeau Says," 16 May 1981 A1.

_____, "Tent vigil pays off for cold landlord," 13 January 1982, A6.

_____, "Class politics make a comeback," David Lewis Stein column, 28 February 1982.

_____, "84% of tenants, homeowners want rent controls, poll says," (The Star Poll), 7 October 1982, A5.

_____, "Another apartment sale now rumoured," 11 November 1982, A16.

_____, "Jobless, widowed mom fears Saudi-Cadillac deal rent hikes," 16 November 1982.

_____, "MPPs demand halt to apartment deal," 16 November 1982, A11.

_____, "Tenants to be protected, Elgie says," 16 November 1982, A1.

_____, "Tenants brave cold to stop pool closing," 17 November 1982, A6.

_____, "Apartments whiz kid in new deal," 18 November 1982, A1.

_____, "Looking happy," 29 January 1983, A4.

_____, "Rosenberg 'insensitive' to tenants—partner," 29 January 1983, A1.

_____, "Rent controls—emotional debate...," 21 February 1983, A1.

_____, "Renters say controls don't protect against illegally high hikes," 21 February 1983, A10.

_____, "Thousands pay unlawfully high rent, probe told," 4 March 1983, A3.

_____, "Pay for fixing rooming houses, province told," 18 August 1983, A6.

_____, "Seven apartments kept empty until landlord can raise rents," 28 August 1984, A6.

The Villager, "Tenants organizing to fight multiple ownership threat," 15 June 1983, 1.

Wall Street Journal, "Surplus Shelter—A glut of rental units grips part of sun belt, may spread elsewhere," 22 July 1983, 1.